NELSON PIQUET

By MIKE DOODSON

PHOTOGRAPHS BY

KEITH SUTTON

NIGEL SNOWDON

HAZLETON PUBLISHING

PUBLISHER
Richard Poulter

EXECUTIVE PUBLISHER
Elizabeth Le Breton

ART EDITOR
Steve Small

PRODUCTION MANAGER
George Greenfield

HOUSE EDITOR
Peter Lovering

PRODUCTION ASSISTANT
Deirdre Fenney

STATISTICS
John Taylor

Black and white photographs contributed by:
Keith Sutton, Nigel Snowdon, Diana Burnett,
International Press Agency, Mike Doodson, Greg Siddle,
Phipps Photographic, David Hutson, Ariane Petitjean,
Charles Briscoe-Knight, Ian House, Dale Rodgers
and Jeff Fisher.

Colour photographs contributed by:
Keith Sutton and Steve Small.

Front cover photograph:
Pascal Rondeau/Allsport.

Back cover photograph:
Keith Sutton.

This first edition published in 1991 by
Hazleton Publishing, 3 Richmond Hill, Richmond,
Surrey TW10 6RE.

ISBN: 0-905138-81-3

Printed in England by BAS Printers Ltd, Over Wallop, Hampshire.

Typesetting by First impression Ltd, Richmond, Surrey.

OTHER TITLES IN THIS SERIES

Nigel Mansell
Niki Lauda
Alain Prost
Gilles Villeneuve
Emerson Fittipaldi
Jochen Rindt
Jim Clark

DISTRIBUTORS

UK & OTHER MARKETS
Osprey Publishing Limited, 59 Grosvenor Street
London W1X 9DA

USA & CANADA
Motorbooks International, PO Box 2
729 Prospect Avenue, Osceola
Wisconsin 54020, USA

AUSTRALIA
Technical Book & Magazine Co. Pty
289-299 Swanston Street
Melbourne, Victoria 3000

Universal Motor Publications
c/o Automoto Motoring Bookshop
152-154 Clarence Street
Sydney 2000, New South Wales

NEW ZEALAND
David Bateman Limited, 'Golden Heights'
32-34 View Road, Glenfield, Auckland 10

With three World Championships behind him and 22 Grand Prix wins, Nelson Piquet could have retired honourably from F1 racing and gone home to Brazil a long time ago. There are a number of people who in 1988 and 1989 advised him to do just that. But Nelson's two victories in Japan and Australia at the end of 1990 demonstrated the truth of his own assertion that he still has plenty of racing in him.

This book sets out to offer an insight into the 'unknown' Nelson and to explain how he has maintained his enthusiasm for a demanding and dangerous activity. He does not fit into any stereotyped racing driver image, and his refusal to take himself seriously has undeniably damaged his reputation, both professionally and personally. Not that Nelson has ever cared about that...

Nevertheless, he represents a little piece of motor racing history, being a champion who raced on equal terms against Fittipaldi, Hunt and Andretti, all of whom had retired from F1 by the early 1980s. He remains unconventional and rather old-fashioned in the detached, highly personal attitude which he brings to winning.

He makes no apology for this, and perhaps there is something to be learned from a man who always put his own satisfaction – and usually his team – before the demands of his sponsors or the media. In 1980 he lost his first chance of the World Championship at Montreal in a first-corner incident with Alan Jones which had all the tension of the Prost/Senna incident at Suzuka ten years later. Instead of making a big issue out of it, Nelson simply got on with his preparations for 1981, when he would defeat Jones. The two men had their differences that year, but ten years later they are able to talk about old times and even to exchange jokes.

Though a mature man with an intensely calculating mind, he is still boyish and innocent in many ways. He can be cruelly honest about the people who surround him, and his scatological sense of humour is not to everyone's taste. At heart, though, he is loyal and passionate, with a great contribution still to make to the sport. These days he doesn't speak out as much as he used to do, but when the conversation is getting serious, the skin stretches white across the bridge of his aquiline nose, and you know that he's going to say something significant.

He can be kind-hearted, too, and although his plans to open an orphanage for deprived Brazilian children have run into bureaucratic delays, he and his mother make significant contributions both in financial and practical terms to various charities for abandoned children in Brazil. Like so much else about himself, these activities are hidden – either because he doesn't want them to become public or because they don't fit in with the image of him that certain elements like to project.

A largely unsympathetic British press, finding him difficult to approach, has depicted Nelson as surly and devious. As a result, the average Silverstone fan tends to remember Piquet not so much for his three World Championships as for his *faux pas*. For instance, he was the helmeted figure who laid into Eliseo Salazar by the trackside at Hockenheim in 1982, under the gaze of a TV camera. Above all, he was the one who 'robbed' Nigel Mansell of two world titles when they were team-mates at Williams. Later, in two barren seasons (1988/89) at Lotus, hardly a Grand Prix passed without James Hunt remarking on BBC television about Nelson's 'lack of motivation'.

Though he couldn't care less what is said or written about him, he does not suffer fools gladly and tends to be gruffly aggressive with questioners who become persistent. If he is enigmatic and mysterious, it is his own fault. Like a first-growth Mouton Rothschild or a solo by Charlie Parker, his qualities are inaccessible and not instantly appreciated. Although they may demand a little time and application to discover, the effort is worthwhile.

In their annual ratings, the editors of *Autocourse* have placed him first only once (after his second title, in 1983) and second twice (in 1980 and 1984). His third World Championship in 1987 earned him only fifth place, yet in 1990 he was given third overall. With a record like this, his professional critics might be well advised to hesitate before describing his performances as inconsistent...

He has concentrated steadfastly on the ultimate objective of any ambitious racing driver, which is to win championships, not individual races. In the heady excitement of a Grand Prix, this is a goal which has eluded many otherwise great and admirable drivers, and it has brought criticism on Nelson for being indolent or uninspired. Yet it is a quality which he has in common with the greatest of them all, Juan Fangio, who did not hesitate to switch teams in F1 and who often drove lacklustre races in sports car events which might otherwise have compromised his F1 endeavours.

Nelson was always adept at economising his efforts. As a result, he is still at the top of F1 racing after more than a decade. Contemporaries like Scheckter and Jones put so much into becoming World Champion that their enthusiasm was soon burned out, but Nelson still looks forward to being on the grid. 'When I'm not driving, I like to get in my boat, fly my plane, or go skiing,' he says. 'I just vanish, so when I come back for a race or testing I am fresh. I don't do things outside racing which need me to make a lot of effort: I do motor racing and I like motor racing.'

Selfish though it may be, his refusal to play to the gallery has brought results – and it has allowed him to maintain his place near the top for so many years. Only a few of Nelson's Grand Prix successes have been won in the crowd-pleasing style which has become associated with the handful of popular heroes thrown up by F1. It's not so much a question of the ends justifying the means as of being aware of the risks and playing the game accordingly.

None the less, there have been some memorable qualifying laps – and the nine 'poles' that he recorded in 1984 equalled the then record held by Lauda and Peterson. When the circumstances are right, when the car is correctly set up and there's a chance of a place on the podium, Nelson's driving takes on a magic sparkle. That glitter vanished in the two 'dead' years with Lotus, but it was back when he joined Benetton in 1990, and never more evident than in the great drive which brought him victory at Adelaide in November 1990, at the age of 38.

The only pressure which really gets to him is that which he places on himself. When other drivers make mistakes, he seizes upon them with glee, and some of his harshest comments have been aimed at fellow World Champions like Prost and Senna when they have slipped up. He particularly enjoys hearing the sort of excuses which are offered by his rivals. 'I don't have to make excuses, like perhaps drivers in big teams [do],' he said in 1984. 'I don't complain because my visor started vibrating or because the gearbox wasn't very good, I admit when I make a mistake. That's my way.'

His impermeability to written criticism makes him a favourite with the competitive Italian media. His practical jokes have become a legend, as one Argentine hack discovered after he headlined an interview in which Nelson confided in him that F1 racing was totally corrupt and that his third World Championship had been 'fixed' beforehand between FISA and the team managers.

Nelson Piquet Souto-Maior was born in Rio de Janeiro on 17 August 1952, the fourth child and third son of a respected MD from the north-eastern state of Pernambuco. Dr Estacio Souto-Maior was elected to Congress and later became Brazil's Minister of Health under João Goulart, the eccentric president whose government was doomed to fall in the military *coup d'état* which ended the country's fragile democracy in 1964. The family moved in 1959 from Rio to Brasilia, the futuristic capital built from scratch in the deep interior of the country. As far as Nelson is concerned, this weird and remote city with its sudden changes of weather remains his home town.

From his father, Nelson says, he got a sense of fair play and honesty. The practical side of his nature came from Dona Clotilde, his mother, who paints, plays piano and even does a little carpentry. She now has an apartment in Rio, bought for her by her son, but she still spends most of the year at the big house in the smart Lago Sul suburb of Brasilia where she raised her family. The two older boys, Alexis and Geraldo, were methodical students who trained for bureaucratic jobs and now work in Brasilia. Genusa, the only daughter, is married and lives in the USA.

By the age of 15, Nelson was running around with a group of kids whose main preoccupation was the internal combustion engine. As the sons of government officials, most of them could afford motorbikes or cars, and Nelson could not wait to join them. But Dr Estacio took a strict line with the boy, who at the age of 12 was already showing an aptitude for tennis, a game at which the doctor himself had excelled. A deal was struck: if he beat his father in a tennis game, Nelson could have a car. Nelson, naturally, applied himself to a stern training schedule. The game took place on his 15th birthday at the Clube de Congresso in Brasilia with the entire family watching. He won the first set 7-5 and the second, with Dr Estacio tiring, by 6-1.

While waiting to get his driving licence, Nelson was sent to America to study at a school which specialised in tennis. He was packed off to northern California, to live with a family in Lafayette. 'It changed complete my life around,' he said in 1988, 'because in Brazil I was the kid of the family and I was used to having maids and servants to do everything for me: in Brazil you don't have to be rich to have servants. In America, as the oldest child, if there was a job to do at home, I had to do it to give a good example. I had to accept a lot of priorities that I did not have in Brazil. For me it was a good situation. I learned a lot of things, I gave a value to a lot of things that didn't have any value for me before. It was a very good year of my life.'

Among the things he had acquired was a grounding in mechanical engineering, picked up in the school workshop. Although he mysteriously lost his English within a few months of returning home, his new-found technical skills would remain with him. Yet he still had no idea of what he was going to do with his life, and racing was certainly not on his list of possible careers. 'When you're 16 or 17, you only think about

Tennis was the first sport for which Nelson showed any aptitude. Although an ankle injury in 1979 slowed his game, he still displays agility and good concentration.

girls. At that age I never knew what I wanted. I never planned anything ahead of me.'

On his return to Brasilia he learned that during his absence the state authorities had raised the legal driving age by one year, and it would be a while before he could drive the blue VW Beetle which was his prize. His brother Alex had fractured his skull in a motor cycle accident and Dr Estacio didn't even want to hear the subject of cars or motor cycles discussed in the house. But Nelson had already bought a kart. He was still fascinated by anything with wheels, and his mechanical knowledge made him an obvious candidate for garage work.

It so happened that one of his companions from the old harum-scarum days was Alex Dias-Ribeiro, who had started a tuning shop in Brasilia known as Camber. Before long, Nelson was in overalls, working on motor cycle engines by day and dreaming of kart victories (and girls, of course) by night.

In the years to come, the youngsters who frequented the workshops at Camber would play important roles in each others' lives. Alex Ribeiro, then racing in Formula Ford, came to Europe in 1976; after some success in F2, he spent a miserable F1 season with March before the team collapsed at the end of 1977. One of the mechanics, Pedro Leopoldo, was himself a hopeful driver who helped to prepare Nelson's cars both in Brazil and Europe; later, he would become a crew member on Nelson's motor cruisers. There was a skinny kid, barely tall enough to see over the steering wheel of a Beetle, who was instantly nicknamed 'Baixo' (Shorty) and never referred to by his real name, Roberto Moreno. Then there was Ribeiro's partner at Camber, Zeca Vassalo, whose sister, Maria-Clara ('Cacala'), would become Nelson's wife in 1976.

In hindsight, the stunts which this group got up to now seem distinctly anti-social. Joy-riding in 'borrowed' cars was a favourite activity, rendered a little more exciting by a self-imposed rule that the vehicle had to be returned to the exact place where it had come from. Ignoring paternal disapproval, Nelson had started racing karts at 17 under the name of Nelson Piket. This was his only concession to family honour, being a deliberate mis-spelling of his mother's maiden name.

On various occasions both his mother's and his sister's Beetles were pressed into service for semi-legal events. 'I also raced Alex's mother's car,' he recalls: 'I changed the engine and the front axle complete with brakes. After the race we worked all night and gave the car back the next day. She had only put it in for a brake service...'

For practice, the gang did not hesitate to use the public highway. Long before many of the buildings planned for outlying areas of the city went up, Brasilia offered an extensive network of loose-surfaced roads which made perfect *ad hoc* circuits. One night, Nelson was racing his Beetle against a friend round one such course when he became aware of lights flashing just over the crest of a hill. Determined to catch the pirate racers, the local police had set up a road block and several officers were lying in wait. Nelson, leading, reacted instinctively with an expert handbrake turn. Departing as rapidly as he had come, he got a shock when the windscreen unexpectedly shattered. In Brasilia, it seems, motor racing is dangerous in more than one sense, because next morning Nelson found a bullet hole in the rear bodywork where a frustrated Federale had loosed off a round. For the record, Nelson's fellow-racer was captured in the incident and spent several uncomfortable weeks in gaol before having his driving licence 'lifted' for a whole year.

*Much poorer (and a lot hairier!) in 1972 than he would
become, Nelson poses with his karting team-mate
Roberto ('Baixo') Moreno and their disreputable VW
Kombi. Note the spelling of 'Piket', who is actually
sitting in his friend's lucky number 19 kart.*

It was kart racing which taught the neophyte Piquet more about car control than those illegal outings. He discovered that events at the kart track in the neighbouring city of Goiânia paid considerably more than those at home. He became a regular and successful competitor at the circuit, usually taking the major prizes which the sons of the city's wealthy landowners and ranchers expected to pick up. Many years later he told of his puzzlement in one important race when he seemed to be lapping the same driver rather frequently. Every time he tried to pass, the other driver seemed determined to put him off the road. Eventually, the rival succeeded, and Nelson decided to report the 'blocker' to the stewards. With his long hair, grease-stained clothes and straggly moustache, he did not cut a very imposing figure. When he went to complain, a fist fight developed, five or six guys against one. Nelson was thrown to the floor, where he was kicked repeatedly in the body and the head. He claims it was the first time he was ever actually saved by a crash helmet.

His first important championship success arrived in 1971, when he won the local (Brasilia) 155 cc kart title. The salary which he received from Camber was never enough to pay for a full-time car racing career, even when topped up with the modest monthly allowance from his father, and he was always short of cash. After several half-hearted attempts at studying subjects as diverse as philosophy and mechanical engineering, the university career which his family wanted for him had ground to a halt. The only thing that mattered was motor racing, and Volkswagens in particular.

In 1972 he was able to borrow an infamous VW-based open sports car built by himself and Ribeiro, the Camber, and won another local title. His obsession with cars made him a virtual recluse. 'He was only interested in learning about practical matters,' recalls the Brazilian journalist Luiz Carlos Lima; 'he never bothered to read anything or to study specific engineering subjects. But he always had an amazing ability to learn quickly. When it came to VWs, there was virtually nothing that anyone could teach him.'

By the beginning of 1973 he was working at Ideal, another tuning shop in Brasilia. In partnership with the owner of Ideal, he was able to scrape together enough cash to buy a year-old Chevrolet Opala saloon car and prepare it for the 12-hour touring car race which was to inaugurate Goiânia's new full-size race track (since used for the World Championship Brazilian motor cycle GP).

Although they finished seventh overall, it was obvious by now that Nelson needed to move on. He was 21 years old, he had a modest number of successes behind him, and he knew that he would have to get himself into a single-seater if he was to progress. The obvious route was Formula Ford, and the logical car to buy was the Heve, by far the most popular chassis of the period. However, Nelson was already a master of the art of lateral thinking, and he concluded that it would be better to look for a different chassis, one that might give him an advantage over everyone who raced the Heve. In late 1973, by a stroke of coincidence (the first of many), he received an invitation to attend a Marlboro party in São Paulo where Emerson Fittipaldi's contract with McLaren would be formally announced. After 12 bumpy hours in the bus, he happened to run into Ronnie Rossi, who had raced in European F3 events.

With several partners, Rossi had set up a workshop in Rio where he planned to build examples of his own single-seater, the Polar. Nelson made the trip to Rio, and sat in the drawing office for four hours watching a draughtsman working on the layout of the car. Even though the Polar was nowhere near the metal-cutting stage, he recognised its potential and put down a deposit. Half of the money belonged to a photographer from Brasilia who had sold some shares to help Nelson financially.

They intended to compete in Formula Ford, but soon after his visit Volkswagen do Brasil announced plans to support a national championship in 1974 for Formula Super Vee, which was already a success in Europe and the USA. This was to be the first of three years which Nelson would spend in Super Vee racing, and soon he was making new friends in São Paulo. Among them was a young architect, Eduardo Prado Jnr, the son of the city's leading corporate lawyer. While Edu had some useful business contacts which would later qualify him to be Nelson's sponsor-finder, he recalls how short of cash Nelson was. 'Ronaldo said he couldn't give Nelson a complete car, because of the cost of labour. But he was prepared to let Nelson have a kit of parts. So Nelson went to live in Rio for six months, and he built it himself.'

The first race of the new championship attracted only 11 competitors. Run in three heats at Goiânia, it was judged to be a great success thanks to some fierce battles between Ingo Hoffmann, Francisco Lameirao and Nelson, who punctured a tyre. Soon afterwards, he got his first close look at the latest F1 cars when the Grand Prix circus arrived in Brasilia to run at the capital's new permanent circuit. It is now history that Nelson made his first contact with the Brabham team at this event. For Herbie Blash, the team's manager, it's all a hazy memory, though. 'I can't remember much except this typical young Brazilian scruffy kid who wanted to be the "gofer" and polish the wheels, which in those days were shiny, and it was a horrible job. He begged our designer Gordon Murray to let him sleep in the garage, to guard the cars at night.' For Nelson, however, the weekend was a landmark. While other young drivers might pine to join Ferrari or Lotus, his time with the team and its drivers, Carlos Reutemann and Wilson Fittipaldi, made him determined to be a Brabham driver one day...

Most of the family were with him in São Paulo a few weeks later for the third race of the Super Vee series at Interlagos when they got the news of Dr Estacio's sudden death. He had collapsed with a heart attack while playing tennis at home, and was already dead by the time Nelson had motored through the night to be with him.

The leading Super Vee drivers had great difficulty taking Nelson seriously. He and Pedro worked on the car together, and he was so short of cash that the budget did not stretch either to a spare engine or more than one set of slicks, so he had to practise on a set of radial tyres. Their only form of transport was his notoriously decrepit VW Kombi, a van concocted from two wrecks. Moreno, a frequent traveller, remembers that the sky was visible through the gaps at the tops of the doors. Somehow, the thing was persuaded to cover the huge distances between the country's race tracks, usually with a trailer behind it. 'He was driving it from São Paulo to Càscavel,' Edu remembers, 'with a trailer and the Super Vee on the back. The Kombi's engine expired, so he just took the FSV engine out, put it in the Kombi and continued. When he got there he took the FSV engine out of the Kombi and raced it.'

As it happened, the engine which had brought the awful Kombi to Càscavel also brought Nelson his first single-seater win. However, it was to be something of a farce, because he tangled with his closest rival at the final corner and the Polar crossed the line backwards, with one wheel hanging off. There was talk of disqualifying him, but eventually he was allowed to keep his win. At the prizegiving that night, the race winner collected his trophy wearing odd shoes, the only pair he could muster. Immediately afterwards, he returned to the task of putting the racing engine back into the Kombi for the long journey home.

The second season of Super Vee, in 1975, found him paying the penalty for a low budget and home preparation. Although he did not win a single race, an impressive tally of pole positions and fastest race laps earned him enough sponsorship to tackle 1976 more professionally, albeit with the same chassis which he had built himself at Polar. He was able to travel to America to get the latest tweaks for the VW engine (still air-cooled in those days) and won six out of the ten races to assure himself of the national title.

Throughout his F1 career, Nelson has acknowledged his debt to Emerson Fittipaldi, the man who urged him to make the trip to Europe and race in Formula 3. In contrast with European drivers, most of whom are steeped in racing lore before they even sit in a racing car, Nelson's reluctance to read newspapers or books has left him with virtually no knowledge of the history of his profession. From his earliest days he had raced because it appealed to his competitive instincts, not for the image that it conferred.

He had followed Emerson's progress on TV as he carried away his world titles of 1972 and 1974 in smooth and virtually faultless style. The younger man held Emerson in such respect (not an abiding Piquet quality!) that he admits to having modelled his own career upon him. 'Emerson was not a fantastically quick driver, but he was very intelligent. He was soft on the car and even when he did not qualify very well he was usually at the finish. He was nearly always on the podium…'

In São Paulo in 1976, Nelson had listened to Emerson and was preparing to follow in his footsteps. Eduardo Prado spoke to some of his father's business contacts and lined up sponsorship from Brastemp and Arno, both companies involved in the household 'white goods' sector. Among Edu's Paulista friends was Carlo Gancia, a wealthy Italian-Brazilian racing fan of his own age whose family has interests in wine and banking, among other things. Edu: 'At the end of '76 we talked to Carlo, and then to the Fittipaldis, and they put us in touch with Ferdinando Ravarotto, an Italian F3 team owner who had worked with Wilson and knew a little bit about Brazilians. Ferdinando arranged a test at Casale in an old Ralt and Nelson flew to Italy. It was bloody cold and when he came back he said the car was rubbish. He still wanted to do F3 but he had decided that he wanted Ronaldo Rossi to build a car for him. Fortunately I managed to speak to the sponsors before he could get to them with this crazy idea, and they insisted we get a British car because it was a much safer investment.'

*The faithful Polar which served Nelson for three
seasons of Brazilian Super Vee racing is seen here in
1976, his championship year.*

On a sizzling hot day in February 1977, Nelson found himself at São Paulo's Viracopos airport with two scruffy suitcases containing virtually all his worldy possessions, bound for Italy. Cacala would follow him later to his new home, a cheap hotel close by the Pederzani brothers' Novamotor workshops in Novara where he would make his base for an attack on the European F3 title. He had ordered a March-Toyota through Ravarotto, and Carlo Gancia had arranged for him to buy an Alfa Romeo road car at a friendly price. With Adilson, a Brazilian gofer to help with the car, he looked ahead to 18 races and a whole new world.

The first race was at the Paul Ricard circuit and, by yet another of the curious coincidences that have followed Nelson's career, Herbie Blash of Brabham happened to be at the circuit during qualifying. 'Someone pointed out that this was the same guy who had looked after our garage at Brasilia a couple of years earlier, and obviously Gordon Murray and I took a lot of interest. We noticed that Nelson had adjusted his lap strap so that he could slide down inside the cockpit and reduce aerodynamic drag as he went down the long back straight. He already knew the importance of power-to-weight and aerodynamics, things that no one else understood in F3 at that time.'

The next race was at the old 14 km Nürburgring, a stern prospect for the Brazilian newcomer. He spun off during qualifying and literally lost his way: he actually had to wait a couple of minutes for the next car to come by before he could rejoin because he couldn't remember which way the track went. At Zolder he experienced perhaps the most bizarre incident of his entire career when he managed to start the race in reverse gear, causing mayhem on the grid behind. He quickly grabbed first and got away without harm. 'I don't think anybody except me realised what had happened,' he says, 'and I was quite happy because the driver behind me got blamed for running into the back of me!'

After finishing third in his fifth race, his suspicions that the March was uncompetitive were confirmed: he would have to get a Ralt. While this was financially inconvenient, it was achieved with a little readjustment. Cacala, who had fallen pregnant, had already gone home. The Alfa was sold and Nelson and his mechanic moved out of the hotel and ended up living in the truck; the tension led to quite a few fist fights. The first race with the Ralt was at Monaco. 'It was wet in the heat and I had a big accident with some Italian who tried to pass me at the swimming pool. After you have been used to racing at circuits like Interlagos, Rio and Monza, coming to Monaco to race is always stupid. I never feel very comfortable here because you can't see what is happening around the corners. But I remember that we camped in the truck, in the tunnel, with a view of the boats on the port. I never dreamed I would have a boat of my own there one day...'

While Piercarlo Ghinzani became the European F3 Champion of 1977, Nelson claimed two victories, at Kassel-Calden and Jarama, to take third place. In the second part of the season, with the Ralt, he amassed more points than anyone else, thanks to an excellent finishing record. Back home, most of his supporters thought the results were good enough to justify a move up to F2. Edu, however, was more cautious. 'Nelson wanted to do F3 in England, and I remember this time I was on his side. He had done pretty well in European F3, but all the Brazilian press had been talking about this new driver Chico Serra, who had won everything in British Formula Ford and was moving up to F3. Chico's mother was a friend of everybody, therefore Serra was the big name in England. So Nelson said that if the press was going to be talking about this guy when he moved into F3, the right thing to do was to do F3 against him, and beat him.'

While this was sound logic, it didn't work out entirely as planned – due to the excellent press service laid on by Serra's ever-loving mother. 'The Brazilian journalists got all the information from her, so the stories in the papers tended to be about Serra's "sensational second place at Mallory Park, etc.", and the only mention that Nelson got was his name in first place on the results panel. But that was why he decided to do F3 – and he ended up winning anyway.'

To begin with it wasn't so easy, though, because Derek Warwick won half a dozen races on the trot. The sponsors in São Paulo had been slow to stump up for another season of F3, and Nelson lost his place in the queue for a new Ralt. Arriving in England only a couple of weeks before the first race, once again he and his mechanic ended up building their own chassis, this time as guests of Ralt chief Ron Tauranac. It was a few weeks before the team really came together as an effective unit, and one of the reasons was the arrival of Greg 'Peewee' Siddle, a tall Australian who in effect took over as team manager. 'It was great to have Peewee around because of his knowledge,' remembers Edu, who had been called in to help for a short period, mainly because he spoke good English. 'He knew where the circuits were, and which hotels to stay at, and he also had a book full of setting-up details so that we knew what wings to run etc.'

Having run Geoff Brabham in F3, Peewee persuaded Tauranac to let the Brazilians move into a disused workshop where they could maintain the car. With virtually everyone in British F3 running a Toyota-engined Ralt in 1978 and given the very short qualifying periods, Nelson concluded that the key to getting an advantage would be to test as often as possible in order to ensure that his car was set up better than anyone else's. Peewee's accounts show that the season cost £66,000, which was certainly less than Serra paid to Ron Dennis, whose Project Four team was running his car. 'Nelson was bloody clever, in ways of setting up the car and driving it,' Peewee recalls. He nominated a victory at Cadwell Park in June as the best race they did together in F3.

It had been raining before the start, and Jimmy Tully of Project Four made the mistake of suggesting to Peewee that they agree to set off on wets, to ensure a close race. The Australian indignantly refused, and when the race started Nelson was on slicks. 'Even then, Nelson knew how to get the absolute optimum out of a racing car in terms of set-up: roll bar, springs, etc. And then the car would go quick, not just for one lap but for the whole race. Well, a lot of people aren't clever like that: their tyres go off and they accept that. But you have to ask *why* the tyres go off, and the reason is that they over-drive the car. But with Nelson, he always had himself covered. Here, I was confident that he would not screw up while the track was drying, and finally we beat Needell, Warwick, Johansson, Rob Wilson, etc.'

Rather typically, Nelson believes that his best race in F3 was an outwardly routine all-the-way victory at Snetterton. The reason: 'I did 20 laps, all within 0.1 second.' Technique over heroics. The die was cast for his F1 future.

There were two F3 championships in the UK that year, and while Nelson won the more important BP title it was 24-year-old Derek Warwick who triumphed in the Vandervell series. BP used their friendly rivalry in some attractive advertisements, and they had a mutual respect. Nelson certainly did not underestimate his British rival, who was still putting in a hard week's work at Warwick Trailers when he was not racing. 'Warwick was an exceptional driver in the wet,' Nelson recalls, 'but he didn't have new ideas on setting up his car like we had.' Those ideas came from the constant testing, which by the end of the year added up to 600 laps of Goodwood in almost weekly sessions. Ron Tauranac wryly remarked that if he had been as dedicated to testing in 1970, with the Brabham F1 team, Jack Brabham would easily have won a fourth World Championship.

Once the R & D programme was working, Nelson won seven races in a row. The winning sequence came to an end on the day before the British GP at Brands Hatch. Nelson and Serra, now arch-rivals, got involved in a shunt at the start which eventually involved 14 cars. History records that Herbie Blash and Gordon Murray – watching the man who was now an unofficial protégé of the Brabham team – pitched in to help him get his spare car ready for the restart.

'I'll never forget the look on Nelson's face,' says Murray. 'He had put the accident right out of his mind and was concentrating completely on getting into the spare car.'

Even though Serra won that race while his rival struggled with his poorly set-up T-car, Nelson's F1 career was about to take a step closer to reality, as Edu recalls. 'We had been watching the F1 practice together when he said, "Do you think I will ever get an opportunity to race one of those things?" I told him that of course he would. He himself obviously wasn't so sure, F1 seemed an impossible dream. But he just happened to say, "Well, I guess I had better call that guy back."'

'That guy' turned out to be Bob Sparshott, whose BS Fabrications team was competing not only in F5000 but also in F1. And the car he wanted Nelson to test was the F1, a McLaren M23. 'Bob had left messages everywhere for Nelson, who had not replied,' says Edu. 'There's a saying that opportunity only knocks once. This may be true, but with a person like Nelson it seems that opportunity knocks…and keeps on knocking, because Bob could so easily have given up on him.'

Meanwhile, the Brazilian's run of F3 successes had not gone unnoticed elsewhere. Mo Nunn, owner of the Ensign F1 team, was having a rather high turnover of drivers. Derek Daly, a front-runner in F2, raced for him at Brands Hatch and Nunn wanted the Irishman to sign an option for 1979. When Daly hesitated, Nelson was invited to race in the German GP. It was only two weeks after Brands Hatch, but Nelson accepted on condition that he could meet his obligations to Sparshott in later races.

With a handful of laps at Silverstone in the BS Fabs McLaren behind him, Nelson approached his first GP with far greater self-assurance than his discussion with Edu two weeks earlier had suggested. The Ensign was a cleverly designed car with several original features: he appreciated its light steering and good traction. Peewee Siddle remembers how relaxed the atmosphere was. 'After the first day, he wasn't even in the race because of a problem with the clutch. He called Cacala from the hotel that night, and when he came off the phone he was just laughing. He had told her about the problems, and apparently she had said, "Yeah, all the new drivers complain. Just pull your finger out and get on with it."'

Nelson did exactly that. He got a big kick out of having qualified faster than three of the Germans in the race (Mass, Ertl and Stuck filled the final three places on the grid) and had made a tremendous start when suddenly he remembered Mo Nunn's pleas not to take any risks. When he backed off, he very nearly got hit from behind. After 31 laps he was forced to retire when the engine – which had sounded rough before the start – blew up.

At Hockenheim, Peewee and Nelson had a meeting with the Fittipaldi brothers about doing F2 in 1979, and they were introduced to a group of BMW personnel which included engine wizard Paul Rosche. But after being button-holed in the pit lane by

*First time out in a Brabham, Nelson drove a third works
BT46 at Montreal. At one stage during qualifying he
was faster than team regulars Lauda and Watson...*

Bernie Ecclestone Peewee knew that F2 would probably not be necessary. 'Bernie
didn't say much,' he recalls; 'he just asked me if Nelson had signed anything for F1 yet.
When I told him no, he just told me to make sure we called him before signing anything.'

Nelson did the Austrian, Dutch and Italian GPs with the BS McLaren, qualifying for
all three and finishing ninth at Monza. Memories of those races were coloured mainly
by the car's heavy steering, which at Zandvoort had him praying for something to go
wrong even before a driveshaft broke on lap 17.

He went to the Canadian GP as a works driver in a Brabham–Alfa which was entered
for him as a third car alongside those of Niki Lauda and John Watson. 'Practice at
Montreal was wet, and there was one point when he was quicker than Wattie and
Niki,' recalls Herbie Blash. 'Bernie came into the debriefing room and I can remember
him telling the other two that they could hang up their helmets, obviously because he
was impressed with the new kid.'

Watson was on his way to McLaren for 1979, and Ecclestone didn't need much per-
suasion from Murray and Blash to sign up the Brazilian. But he did not let his
enthusiasm run away with him when it came to paying a retainer. 'Nelson stayed with
me in my house for a while,' Herbie recalls, 'and when I took him down to the pub he
would ask for a Coca-Cola because he had no money at all. At first he was riding a
push-bike to and from the factory because he had no money for a car. Later he started
going to the car auctions, and I remember that he got himself a Mini and polished it
up and tried to sell it.'

*Seen here at the Österreichring, where he spun off on a
sodden track, Nelson built up his arm muscles in three
GPs with the BS Fabs McLaren M23 thanks to its
heavy steering.*

Gordon Murray's new car for 1979 was the BT48, designed around the V12 version of the 'boxer' Alfa Romeo. Early in the new year the team stopped off for testing at Interlagos *en route* to Buenos Aires, but Nelson's hopes of getting a run were dashed when the rear brakes failed while Lauda was getting up to speed, and the car speared through the catch-fences.

In the Argentine race, Watson's McLaren clashed with Scheckter's Ferrari at the Esses immediately after the start. In the aftermath, the new boy in the Brabham collided with the Ferrari. He was trapped by his feet, and at the track hospital it was found that Nelson had cracked a bone in his ankle. The investigation took quite a while because Nelson lay on the examination table pleading with the medics to remove his shiny new overalls without cutting them. Even though those fireproofs were a perk from Parmalat, the uniform was probably the most expensive personal possession he had ever owned...

It was asking too much for the bone to be healed in time for the Brazilian GP two weeks later. Both he and the team's sponsor were determined that he be on the grid for his home race, though. Having done enough to qualify, the car went to the line with a few litres of fuel in the tank, on qualifying tyres, and Nelson received a mild shot of anaesthetic in the foot. Clay Regazzoni spared him the task of inventing a reason for retiring early when he tried to defend his 12th place too vigorously on lap four. The extra braking effort sent a stab of pain up Nelson's leg, and he instinctively lifted off, damaging a front wing on the rear of the Swiss driver's Williams.

Thereafter, the Brabham team's season developed into a depressing list of retirements. Lauda picked up four points, Piquet three for his only finish with the Alfa car, a distant fourth at Zandvoort. In August it had already been decided to ditch the inconsistent and unreliable Alfa V12 in favour of a Ford V8-powered car. The BT49 was ready in a record 55 days, but Lauda stepped out of his new car halfway through the Canadian GP meeting at the end of September. Nelson would miss the Austrian, from whom he had learned a lot. Their only public clash came at Hockenheim, where Niki got a bit miffed about Nelson being given a set of his qualifying tyres. The two men would remain close, even after Lauda's return to racing in 1982.

'I suppose [our friendship] goes back to being together at Brabham when I came into Formula 1 [in 1978],' Nelson reflected in 1984. 'Niki always treated me very good: he left racing, then he came back – and we talk a lot about boats, aeroplanes, life: those sorts of things. He is a very straightforward person. He has nothing to hide. He never talks about you behind your back. He has a very good character.'

Niki got something out of the friendship, too. Perhaps the most important thing was learning how to relax, something at which the Brazilian is so expert. Even when Nelson was under the most severe pressure, his tendency was to go to sleep. He has been known to do it even when sitting on the grid, in his car, waiting for the start after some delay.

*Having clearly overcome the nausea which then affected
him on street circuits, Nelson's first GP win at
Long Beach is saluted by Emerson Fittipaldi (left),
the man who had persuaded him to go to Europe three
years earlier.*

For 1980, Nelson would have to assume Lauda's role as team leader, with precious little support from the renta-drivers (Ricardo Zunino and then Hector Rebaque) employed by Ecclestone. Yet virtually from the first race, the year was to be a duel between the Brazilian and Australia's Alan Jones, leading the Williams effort. For Nelson, the most glorious moment came at round four, Long Beach, where he started from pole position and led all the way. Ten years later, he still remembers the chisel-nosed Brabham as the best-handling F1 car he ever raced. 'I knew it was good in qualifying when all four tyres blistered at exactly the same moment. *That* is good set-up...'

*Long Beach 1980: from pole position (his first), Nelson
grabbed the lead from René Arnoux's Renault at the
first hairpin and led all the way to take a classic maiden
win in F1.*

Right: *With Gordon Murray, the brains and guiding*
spirit at Brabham during Nelson's seven-year tenure.
'Gordon always understood, even when I got angry and
went over the top.'

'Like riding a motorbike round your apartment' is
Nelson's description of driving at Monaco. Bernie
Ecclestone evaluates the cost of this 'off' during practice
for the 1980 GP, in which Nelson finished third.

A convincing victory in the Italian GP at Imola in 1980
kept Nelson in the hunt for the World Championship
with Alan Jones.

*Brands Hatch, 1980. Alan Jones is weighed down by
trophies, leaving Nelson to get started with the
champagne. Third man Carlos Reutemann watches
apprehensively.*

In the first 13 of the season's 14 races, he failed to pick up a top-six placing only twice. Although Alan Jones got ahead on points in mid-season, victories for Nelson in Holland and Italy put him in with a fighting chance of taking the title in the final round at Montreal. He took pole position from Jones, but his side of the grid was dirtier than the racing line where Jones would start. On the grid, Bernie Ecclestone pretended to offer a bribe to Didier Pironi, the third-fastest qualifier, if he would see Jones off the road.

Going down to the first turn, a flat-out right-hand swerve, Jones was half a length in front. When he moved right to take up his line for the following left-hander, Piquet did not flinch. The two cars touched, and Jones's engine cover flew into the air as Piquet slammed into the retaining wall. In the ensuing chaos, half a dozen cars were wrecked and the race was stopped. The Williams was repairable, but the Brabham's steering was too badly damaged: for the restart, Nelson had to take the spare car. And although he led the race when it got under way 90 minutes later, his engine – which had been 'buzzed' during qualifying but not changed – blew up. Alan Jones was the 1980 World Champion.

Herbie Blash still feels bitter that someone did not have the foresight to change the engine in the spare car overnight. The failure to do so was the responsibility of someone whose tenure at Brabham – and in F1 racing – would not last very much longer. But whose fault had the accident been? Did Jones act deliberately to cut off his rival? The Brabham/Piquet faction, led by Herbie, maintains to this day that Nelson was pushed off. But Jones, who would surely have confessed by now if there had been any hanky-panky, is firm. 'I was in front. His front wheel hit the engine cover of my car, so he must have been behind. The guy in front has a right to the racing line.'

Nelson has no ill feeling towards Jones. He doesn't often look back, especially on old motor races. 'By six o'clock on Sunday evening, the race is dead and buried. It doesn't matter whether I won it or lost, I just forget it. If I let myself get eaten up inside by thinking about it, I would have retired years ago.' It was so in Canada: loading luggage into his hire car outside the Hyatt hotel the following morning, he showed no regrets. 'I was not ready to be World Champion,' he said unemotionally. 'I can do it again next year.'

*Alan Jones holds the lead moments after the restarted
1980 Canadian GP has got under way. Using his spare
car, Nelson slipped in front and held the lead until its
high-compression DFV qualifying engine blew up.*

Right: *With Sylvia Tamsma, mother of Nelson Jnr and Kelly.*

Not many drivers could claim to be close friends with Nelson, but an important exception was Dutchman Jan Lammers.

Nelson sits in the superbly effective Brabham BT49. 'It blistered all four tyres at the same moment,' he said in tribute to its excellent chassis balance.

Bernie Ecclestone once said that it was Nelson who had deserved to be World Champion in 1980 and Alan Jones in 1981. Certainly Jones was in virtually unbeatable form in his final year of F1, but his Williams suffered from a stupid fuel-feed problem which wasn't sorted out until it had cost him two or three races.

Now running on Michelin tyres, Brabham and Nelson also threw away a couple of races. In Rio, under a warm tropical rainstorm, his car was switched from grooved tyres to slicks as it sat on pole position. The rain never let up and Nelson was to become the butt of countless jokes suggesting that he should think twice if he was ever tempted to become a TV weather man. Herbie Blash has since revealed that this barmy decision was in fact taken by the same team member who had failed to order a change of his T-car's engine in Montreal.

Piquet made no mistakes in Argentina, where he dominated with the help of Gordon Murray's brilliantly conceived self-adjusting ride-height mechanism, which was months in advance of anybody else's attempts to compensate for FISA's ludicrous '6 cm' skirt rule. There was ill feeling from Frank Williams about Murray's technology; even more seriously, a spectator flung an orange which barely missed Nelson's head as he sped by at 150 mph.

The San Marino GP at Imola very nearly didn't happen because of FISA's notorious wrangle with the teams over aerodynamic skirts. Nelson got the better of Pironi's Ferrari to win a splendid race, and he was set to win again at Monaco – until he thumped the barrier while lapping Tambay's Theodore. He acknowledges that the excellent balance of the Brabham was superior to the understeery Williams, but refuses to accept that he was pressured into the mistake by Jones, who was cutting into his lead. 'I was driving comfortably, and the misunderstanding with Tambay caused the accident, nothing else.'

With Jacques Laffite making an unexpected charge, Nelson's third and last victory of the 1981 season was posted in Germany. Going into the final race, at Las Vegas, Carlos Reutemann had a one-point advantage, 49 to 48, over Nelson.

John Watson says that Reutemann was totally demoralised. 'He drove the entire weekend looking in his mirrors,' says Wattie, 'and when he saw Nelson come up to pass, he simply gave in.' Nelson greeted the unfortunate Reutemann's gesture of defeat more graphically as he drove home gently to take fifth place and two points. 'He just open the legs,' he said in the garage as he peeled off the tacky crown which Caesar's Palace casino had awarded him.

Becoming World Champion did not swell Nelson's head, although he was determined that it would have the opposite effect on his wallet. In 1979 Bernie paid him nothing. In return for ID on his overalls he got $27,000 from Brastemp, one of his F3 sponsors, and topped it up with the £25,000 which had been released by selling off the F3 car and equipment. But his principal income came from the association with BMW which would eventually lead to the title in 1983.

BMW's Procar series, in which a selection of F1 stars and 'gentleman-drivers' raced BMW M1 coupés in events which supported the European GPs, paid well. In the second year of the series, 1980, Nelson had the consolation of beating Alan Jones to the overall title. The Procar earnings allowed him to buy a small yacht, and by 1981 he was thinking about something much bigger. He ordered a 22-metre motor yacht, the *Gostosa* (Portuguese for 'tasty'), which would become his hideaway between races.

He was already residing in millionaires' territory, for after one English winter living in a rented semi at Claygate, near the Brabham factory in Surrey, he was happy to move to Monaco.

Finishing second to his chum Roberto Moreno (with hats) in the 1981 Australian GP for Formula Pacific cars at Bob Jane's one-mile Calder circuit. Nelson didn't take the race too seriously after he learned that the Australian tax man wanted a 35 per cent slice of his fee!

In 1980 his F1 earnings were up to $50,000 – still virtually nothing even by the standards of that era. 'He was totally comfortable with that at the time,' recalls Peewee Siddle, 'although I was not. Long-term, his theory was more correct than mine, because he knew that Bernie and Gordon could offer him the championship. And that put him in a very strong position from '81 onwards.'

Indeed, in August 1981 Nelson opened negotiations with McLaren for the drive alongside John Watson which eventually went to Andrea de Cesaris. It didn't happen – for reasons that were typically his. 'The thing that really annoyed him was the multi-page contract that Ron Dennis wanted him to sign,' says Peewee. 'He told Ron, "Look, I've just driven for a guy for three years, and our whole contract was written on one sheet of paper." Nelse actually picked up the contract and walked out. Ron had to chase after him and bring him back. I guess Ron just never rubbed up with Nelson. He regarded us – Nelson and me – as a bunch of hillbillies.'

Ron Dennis's offer was $800,000 for 1982. Nelson was holding out for $1.2 million from Bernie, and eventually he got it. It allowed him to become a big spender, and he already had some help. Her name was Sylvia Tamsma, a German-Dutch photographic model who had already been seen on the arm of several F1 personalities. It was in a Long Beach disco on the night of his first F1 victory that Nelson rescued her from her companion Giulio de Angelis (father of Elio). Although Nelson was (and remains) close to his son Geraldo ('Geepee'), the marriage to Cacala was over. Sylvia's hard-headed ambition was much more attractive than Cacala's subdued hominess: he admitted that a bit of push was just what he needed at this important stage in his life.

Professionally speaking, the real push in 1982 would come from BMW. Right from the first appearance of Renault's 'yellow teapot' in July 1977, Bernie Ecclestone and FOCA had demonstrated their firm opposition to the French company's exploitation of the regulations which permitted 'supercharged' 1.5-litre engines. By the end of 1980, though, even Ecclestone had to concede that the future lay with the new turbo technology. When BMW approached him, he agreed on a technical collaboration which the German company hoped would result in a BMW-engined Brabham being ready to race in 1981.

Nelson already had good contacts with several of BMW's personnel. He had contested two 1000 km races at the Nürburgring in works BMW M1s, each time with Hans Stuck co-driving, and they had won outright in 1981, the year that the race was stopped following Herbert Müller's fatal accident.

As soon as the first turbo-powered F1 Brabham 'hack' was available, he was there to test it. The car ran regularly throughout 1981, and even made a public appearance in practice at the British GP. But as BMW's *Rennleiter* (racing chief) Dieter Stappert recalls, the BMW board of directors was even more anxious than Nelson to see it in action.

'Bernie said it would be too difficult and too complicated to run two different types of car at the same time,' Stappert recalls, 'so we decided to postpone our race debut until the first GP of 1982 at Kyalami. I could understand, because I had already been in racing for a long time. But it was very difficult to explain all this to the board of BMW and to the German public. Anyway, we got over that...'

The practical difficulties of getting the BMW engine reliable were not so easy to

surmount. 'The first time we tried the new Bosch Motronic engine management was at the end of 1981, in the pouring rain at Donington. That was a great test for us, because the Motronic worked perfectly. I remember Nelson coming into the pits when it was so late in the day that all you could see on the car was the turbo glowing red on the left-hand side. He just said, "perfect, perfect, perfect".

'The Bosch people were there, of course, so we told them to carry on their development programme but first to make three copies of the box we had used at Donington, because we knew it was working well. That way we could carry on the chassis testing. But somehow Bosch screwed it up. Although we did not find out until much later, apparently in measuring the box they blew it up in a little cloud of smoke. And they couldn't get it back together.

'That was bad enough, but what made it worse was that they would not tell us what had happened. They insisted it was the same, even when Nelson complained. We then went testing at Paul Ricard, one of the most difficult times in my life, because in two weeks we blew something like 17 engines. Nelson was doing all the turbo testing, whenever there was a car for him to run, while Riccardo [Patrese] had the Cosworth-engined car, and every day it seemed he broke the lap record. I was amazed how Nelson stuck to the turbo test. You must remember that he was the new World Champion, but not once did he go to Gordon Murray and ask to be given the Ford car so that he could do five laps and beat Riccardo's time. No way. He couldn't care less about Patrese's lap records.

'But right from the first laps, he could tell that the Bosch system was not the same as it had been at Donington. "It *must* be different," he told them, "it's nothing like as good as it was at Donington, I am 100 per cent sure." Only after nine or ten blow-ups did they confess what had happened. You cannot imagine how much money that cost us.'

For Kyalami, BMW played safe and took engines fitted with mechanical fuel injection pumps. The BMW board was now looking for positive results at last, and the last thing they wanted to read about was the famous drivers' strike which caused the cancellation of the first day of qualifying.

'A lot of people got upset with Nelson then, because he was the driving force behind the strike, with Niki,' Stappert recalls. 'I did not know Nelson as well then as I was to know him later, but I was sure there must have been a serious reason which at that moment I did not understand. I took all my courage in my hands and went up to Bernie and told him the same. Right there in pit lane, he screamed at me as though I was a little boy. It made me feel so sick that I just turned around and left.'

After some more histrionics from Ecclestone, who at first refused to let Nelson practise on the second day of qualifying, the new Brabham BT50-BMW only just missed pole position. 'The engine characteristics were still very rudimentary,' confesses Stappert, 'and although that car was very quick on the straight, you really needed someone brave to drive it. In the race, Nelson made a mess of the start. Trying to catch up, he missed the braking-point at the end of the straight and slid straight on. Patrese also stopped early with an engine problem or something.'

Nelson and Sylvia spent a week with Stappert in Austria at the ski World Championships on their return from Kyalami, and a lasting friendship was established. The genial but practical Stappert found a great ally in Nelson, who was as dedicated to making the BMW turbo a success as anyone in the engine shop. They both wanted to test and race the new car intensively, to speed up progress. But Ecclestone had a sponsor, Parmalat, to placate. He wanted BMW to withdraw the turbo in Brazil and Long Beach, the next two races, and very cleverly managed to outwit Stappert at a lunch which he arranged with Herr Schönbeck, one of BMW's board members, soon after the team returned from South Africa.

Stappert: 'They made a press release saying that the engine was too strong, and Brabham needed to improve their brakes, etc. That was all bullshit. We continued testing but we always had trouble with the electronic management. Then there was a test in April when we went to Zolder. Bosch had four or five different boxes, and all five of them worked. Nelson would do five laps, everything was OK, then five more with another box.

'After the test in Zolder Nelson called Bernie from the telephone in the little office in the pit lane. They were shouting at each other, apparently because Bernie wanted to discourage Nelson from running the turbo. But Nelson insisted that he wanted to use the turbo. He came out of the office and immediately told our engine chief Paul Rosche and myself, "Listen, I am prepared to stick my neck out, but I now rely on you to convince your BMW board to run only the one turbo car for me."

'The funny sequel to this took place on the day after I got home, only a few minutes after I had got Herr Schönbeck to agree to Nelson's proposal. I was still in Schönbeck's office when Bernie rang, and Schönbeck switched on the loudspeaker so I could hear what was being said. Frankly, I could not believe my ears as I listened to Bernie telling Schönbeck that he personally had managed to persuade Nelson to run just one engine.'

Brabham reverted to the Ford-engined car for the next two GPs. The first of them was in Rio, where Nelson scored the victory which he still likes to look back on more than any other, even though it was later taken away from him. Considering that he actually pressured Gilles Villeneuve into making a mistake which handed him the lead, that is hardly surprising.

Once again, though, the critics had a field day with Nelson. Because he collapsed on the podium as he received his trophies, it was assumed that he was in poor physical shape. 'The problem was I didn't want to go on the podium, because I was high,' Nelson recalls. 'People forget that I drove 28 laps one metre from the exhaust of the Ferrari, a turbo car, and there was gas and heat coming at me all the time: I finished the race very good,' he insists.

It should also be mentioned that the cockpit windscreen had been replaced on the night before the race with a slightly higher one. The reduced flow of air affected both drivers equally. As Nelson gently points out, 'Riccardo was very well prepared and he fell off the road ten laps before me.'

Ten days later, FISA announced that Nelson would be deprived of his win, and Williams driver Keke Rosberg of second place. The federation disapproved of the water-bottle 'brake cooling' systems adopted by certain British teams which enabled them to 'top up' before post-race scrutineering and reach the minimum weight limit.

In an attempt to even the score with the ever-improving turbo teams, the constructors

A staggering achievement and a momentary collapse on the top step of the podium at Rio, 1982. Even though both he and Keke Rosberg were later disqualified in the infamous 'water tank' dispute, Nelson still regards this as his greatest victory.

Bottom: Moment of truth at Rio as Nelson darts for the inside when a desperate Gilles Villeneuve slides wide (seconds later, he nearly collected the Brabham). Despite breathing Ferrari fumes for 29 laps, Nelson actually showed greater stamina than team-mate Patrese.

*Grim looks on the podium at Montreal, June 1982.
The joy of Nelson's breakthrough victory for BMW
took second place to mourning for Ricardo Paletti, who
died in a startline accident.*

involved had used the 'topping-up' principle for more than a year. If the blame for this farce belonged anywhere, it was with FISA, for its fuzzy rules and incompetent administration. The decision to clamp down on Piquet and Rosberg after Brazil, and to do so retrospectively, went against all natural justice. It led directly to the British boycott of the next race, at Imola.

Exploiting the imprecisely written F1 rule book was a temptation that Brabham, above all others, found difficult to resist over the years. It was not until 1987 that regular checks on weight were instituted – or even that a rule was brought in to require a minimum weight under anything other than race conditions.

It is ironic that the two engineers now employed by FISA to check on such irregularities are both former Brabham employees, indeed both former mechanics on Nelson's Brabhams. As Herbie Blash recalls, there was a time in '80 and '81 when the Brabham crew were up to every trick in the book. 'Our cars were always under weight. We had a 50-kilo seat which needed two people to lift it. Just before the end of the practice session we would swap the seats because they didn't weigh the cars until afterwards then. Also, we had a rear wing that was so heavy it needed three people to lift it.

'The way the rules were at that time, there was no way of checking. But I remember one time, racing in Argentina, when we had the lightweight seat in, and the car stopped on the circuit. We had to send two guys staggering out with the heavy seat. It was diabolical the things we got up to. But Nelson was always determined to have what has been described as "the unfair advantage", and he encouraged it.'

After the disqualification in Brazil and the non-appearance at Imola, the patience of the BMW board was stretched very thin. At Detroit in June the decision to run only one BMW-engined car, put into effect at Monaco after two BT50s had raced in Belgium, seemed to have gone horribly wrong. Nelson failed to qualify.

'That was partly our fault,' confesses Stappert, 'because the engine stopped on the far side of the circuit, and by the time he got back the qualifying was over. The next day it was pouring with rain...Gordon Murray was completely flattened. He could not believe that one of his cars had not qualified. He insisted that the only way to go was to stop racing the turbo and go testing. I said, "No, Gordon, this is not possible. The board will not accept it. We have to race in Montreal in one week's time."'

After a series of threats and counter-bluffs, Murray agreed to Stappert's pleadings. With the BMW sounding tremendous Piquet went into the lead from Arnoux's Renault after eight laps. Stappert was on cloud nine. 'For me, the world could have ended there and then: after the hard time we had been given in Detroit, we had shown the people back home in Germany that we had a competitive combination.'

Stappert got a big shock ten laps from the end of the race when Bernie Ecclestone started to gather his things together in readiness to go to the airport for the evening flight home to London. Nelson was leading, but Patrese in the Ford car was not too far behind him in second place. Stappert could not believe that even Ecclestone would walk away from a race that his drivers were about to win in 1-2 order. 'Feeling a bit helpless, I said, "but what do I do if Patrese catches Nelson and they start fighting for the lead?" He just turned round and said, "Do what you like!"'

*After leading comfortably at the Österreichring in 1982,
Nelson's chances evaporated when the valvegear broke.*

Viewers of the BBC's transmission from Germany saw quite a fight about the lead ... except that it wasn't on the track. Nelson Piquet found himself a little piqued after losing the lead when a manoeuvre to pass Eliseo Salazar's ATS went wrong, and in front of millions of television viewers across the world, lost his temper with the Chilean. The promotion of Grand Prix racing's 'good, clean image' was completed by front page photographs and cartoons in several daily newspapers ...

Reproduced courtesy of Autosport. Copyright: FOCA.

*This outburst of physical abuse against Eliseo Salazar
at Hockenheim in 1982 earned more publicity for
Nelson than his 1981 World Championship had done.
In fact, he was well aware of the TV camera recording
the incident…*

That victory virtually saved BMW's participation in F1. However, a string of mishaps and mechanical failures prevented Nelson from finishing six of the remaining eight races. Surely the most spectacular retirement was the one at Hockenheim, where BMW was particularly anxious for a good finish. Instead, TV spectators around the world saw Nelson taken off the road at one of the chicanes by the ATS of Eliseo Salazar. Once out of his car, Nelson laid into the unfortunate Chilean with fists and feet, right under the gaze of a TV camera.

Although no lasting physical harm was done, the incident added nothing to the Piquet image. However, Peewee Siddle offers a reason for the outburst, if not an excuse.

'It's amazing how many people have seen that incident on TV and simply condemned Nelson. But you have to get to know behind this story to understand the full implications. Nelson had gone to Thruxton for an F3 race in 1979, and he was driving home, alone, in his Mercedes when he saw a guy just walking down the main road towards Andover with a briefcase in his hand.

'It was a pretty bleak sort of Thruxton day, so Nelson stopped to pick the guy up. It was Salazar, who had arrived in England to go F3 racing, almost literally with nothing except a briefcase full of money. That night Nelse told me about this guy and asked me to help him. We had quite a lot of contact, and I actually helped him to buy a road car.

'Basically, as a person he was pleasant enough, but we didn't like the way he tried to come on. I have never let anyone race one of my cars just because of the money he offered, and I did not want Salazar on those terms. But I introduced him to someone who would do the job for him, and he was on his way.

'What irked Nelson at Hockenheim was that Salazar, the guy he had literally picked up at the side of the road, was totally to blame. Nelson told me that his first reaction had been to head-butt him in the chest. But he decided not to do that, because he realised it might break his ribs. So then he vented his anger in the way that the world saw in such detail.

'To this day, though, like so many of the other things which have generated so much criticism, he doesn't regret what he did,' says Peewee, a passionate defender. His only criticism of the champion is that he hasn't given enough time to the sport. 'He just doesn't enjoy signing autographs and meeting fans. It makes him uncomfortable. But I think he will put a lot back into the sport when he retires. I doubt that he will do a Jody Scheckter and virtually disappear from view…'

Now resident in Australia again, Peewee believes that his friend is badly misrepresented in the Australian newspapers, which in racing matters take their lead from the British press and TV. 'When Nelson has got his guard down, he's a human being who can do things that we would all like to do if we had half a chance,' he says. 'We all play practical jokes, and we are not ashamed of it. But people have to understand that Nelson likes to switch off and go into his mode – which has always been there – and switch on to another level.'

This mysterious side to Nelson Piquet may have its origins in his ancestry. Very early in his career, Carlo Gancia dubbed him 'the Indian', because he had come from Brazil's vast interior. But Nelson believes that there is true Amazon Indian blood in his veins, acquired through his father's family in Pernambuco. Like a Latin, his face instantly reflects emotional reaction. But the dark, limpid eyes conceal a personality which is, and remains, unfathomable to all, including his closest friends.

*Judging from the expressions here, Nelson is probably
recounting one of his notoriously off-colour anecdotes to
an amused Roberto Moreno (centre) and slightly
uncomfortable Greg ('Peewee') Siddle, the man who
had supervised their early careers.*

Of his three World Championships, Nelson's 1983 success is the one which gave him the most satisfaction. It was a true 'family' effort by the Brabham team and by BMW, whose technicians saw an opportunity to beat Renault at the end of the season, and grabbed it. With four races to go, and 36 points still available, the Régie rashly plastered billboards across France with posters to congratulate Alain Prost, 'our champion'. Granted, Alain had built up a 14-point advantage in the championship. But the adulation was to be proved horribly premature…

Nelson would win only three GPs that year (against Prost's four). One of them was a second consecutive victory in his 'home' race, at the Jacarepaguá circuit in Rio which would be renamed the 'Autodromo Nelson Piquet' in his honour in 1988. Gordon Murray's new car, the BT52, was a completely new design to meet the emergency 'flat bottom' regulations imposed at the end of 1982. With its small fuel tanks, the BT52 was also able to take full advantage of the mid-race refuelling ploy which Murray had introduced in mid-1982.

Fearing the bad publicity which would fall on his employers if a refuelling stop were to end in a bonfire, Renault's Gérard Larrousse would not at first allow his team to use this tactic. Although Renault eventually adopted fuel stops, by then the French had probably sacrificed the two or three points which would have been enough to defeat Brabham, BMW and Piquet. As Nelson himself commented, 'it was not Prost who lost the championship, it was Renault who threw it away.'

Opposite page: *A decisive factor in Brabham's 1983
success was the pit stop tactics introduced by senior
engineer Gordon Murray, seen leaping out of the way at
the British GP after the crew has refuelled and re-shod
Nelson's car.*

*Nerfed off by Prost in a desperate move, Nelson rolls to
a halt at Zandvoort, 1983. It was, in fact, a decisive lost
opportunity for the Frenchman, whose Renault retired
with accident damage less than one lap later.*

But Prost's driving was not entirely fault-free in 1983, and the turning-point of the season came at Zandvoort, where a rather desperate overtaking move by the Frenchman pushed Nelson out of the race while they were disputing the lead. Prost continued, but had covered less than one lap when a front wing, damaged in the incident with the Brabham, suddenly folded under and sent the Renault understeering off the track.

Afterwards, a flock of pressmen descended on Nelson and tried to sympathise with him for an incident in which he was clearly the innocent party. He rejected the sympathy, for he knew that on that day his car was not the equal of the Renault. 'Prost could have chosen his moment to pass me, and I am sure he knew it,' he said. 'Instead, he tried to pass me at the wrong place, and he put us both out. Without that, he would have had three points more than me today.'

With that 14-point 'cushion' established before Zandvoort, Renault's technicians were instructed to 'freeze' the specification of their engine. BMW's Paul Rosche pounced on this weakness to press on with his own development programme, squeezing more and more power each week from the little four-cylinder stock-block.

Aided splendidly by his team-mate Riccardo Patrese, Nelson led all but three laps at Monza, where Prost's turbo failed. In the European GP at Brands Hatch, he beat Prost hands-down, despite a scare during the pit stop when an air gun failed. Suddenly, Prost's advantage had been cut from 14 points to two. The title would be decided in the final race at Kyalami.

*A clear victory at Monza, though only his second win
of the season, put Nelson within five points of Prost,
whose Renault retired with another turbo failure.*

Prost never looked more than second-best in South Africa. Renault's technical equality with Brabham-BMW was gone, and he was resigned to defeat, even if he finished. When a turbo failure forced him to stop, it was just a matter of Nelson bringing the Brabham home safely. Expecting that it might be necessary to out-psyche Renault, Gordon Murray had started both drivers on soft tyres and with light fuel. Nelson built up a 30-second lead in 28 laps before his stop: he first waved Patrese through, then de Cesaris's Alfa. One or two hearts fluttered in the Brabham pit when his BMW seemed to be misfiring. In fact, he had cut back the boost to almost nothing as he cruised to the third place which would give him the title.

The first man to congratulate Nelson when he completed his slowing-down lap was Prost. Soon afterwards there was a delightful gesture from Frank Williams, who finally defused any residual tension from Nelson's old feud with Alan Jones by planting the number 1 on Nelson's car in the pit lane. 'It would never have done to have had a French car win the championship,' he muttered.

Bernie Ecclestone, as usual, was an early departure, looking amazingly disgruntled for someone whose driver was about to win the world title for the second time in three years. In fact, he left instructions for Nelson to be bollocked for letting de Cesaris through.

The new champion got back at his boss in the press room, where he was thumping his knee in delight as he chatted with the journalists. 'I wanted to win [the championship] this year even more than the first time,' he said. 'In 1981 I won it for Ecclestone, for my family and for the people who had shown their faith by taking me into F1 straight from F3.

'This time I won for *me*. We were a long way behind on points, so we said, "OK, we'll win the three or four last races and get the championship." We planned it all, we did it – and it was *fantastic*. What I can say is that every time Brabham gave me a chance to win the championship, I never let them down. I never lost the championship by a few points. And that makes me feel very good.'

There was a nasty postscript still to come when rumours began to circulate that BMW had used fuel with illegal additives to boost its engines' power in those crucial last four races. A sample taken from Nelson's car at Kyalami was sent for analysis, and the eventual FISA report showed that it met all the requirements. BMW's Paul Rosche insisted that there had been no cheating, and he was upset to discover that part of the sample had found its way into the hands of Elf, Renault's fuel supplier.

The defeated challenger was in no doubt about the propriety of the win, though. In one of the tough statements that would cost him his job at Renault, Alain Prost gallantly observed that 'the best car won the championship – and Nelson was the best man to drive it'.

Although Nelson would stay with Brabham and BMW through two more seasons, the World Championship was about to be dominated by McLaren, TAG-Porsche and the driving talents of Niki Lauda and Alain Prost. In 1984 Nelson claimed nine pole positions – a record which he shared with Lauda and Peterson until Ayrton Senna topped it in 1988 with 13 poles – but he won only two races.

The 1984 season brought a change to Nelson's life when he split with Sylvia Tamsma. More precisely, Sylvia ceased to be the 'official consort', for she was

Everyone except Bernie Ecclestone was happy with Nelson's third place at Kyalami in the last race of 1983. Here the new champion salutes BMW and his crew as he completes the slowing-down lap.

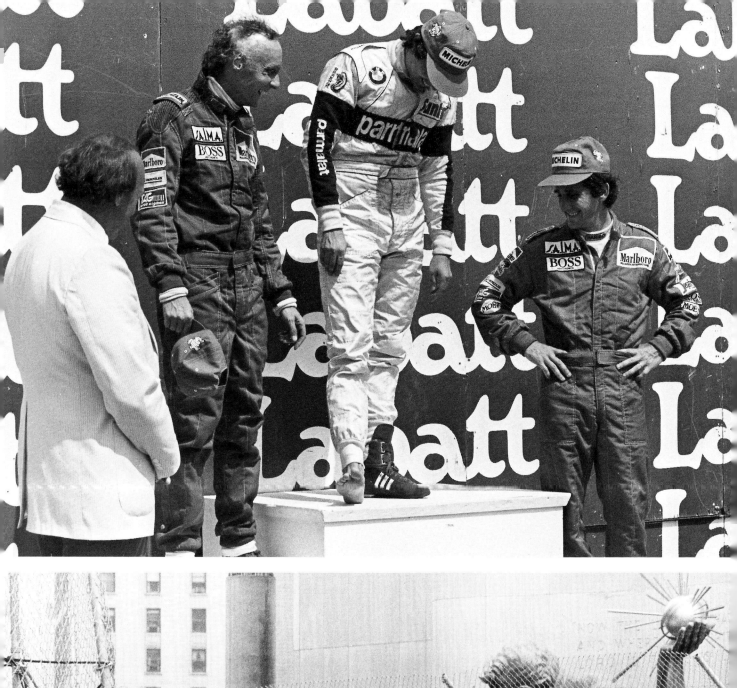

subsequently to become the mother of two of his children, Nelson Jnr (born 1986) and Kelly (born 1988). The new travelling companion was to be Emanuela Enfi, a teenage Italian model who was employed by Piaggio to present the scooters which the company was awarding to the pole position winners.

As Nelson joked, 'I didn't just get nine scooters and the girl that year, I also got $47,000 in cash for being on pole position so many times.'

Despite those several consolations, Nelson was unhappy with developments on the engine side. He felt that BMW, under pressure from TAG-Porsche, was trying to squeeze too much power from its production-based 'four', but Paul Rosche blamed a fall in the quality of the components supplied by outside contractors.

The speed of the new BT53 was awe-inspiring, and on the Jukskei Straight at Kyalami Renault clocked it at 211 mph. Equally impressive were the TV pictures of the two Brabhams raising showers of sparks from their new titanium skid-plates, another Gordon Murray 'first'. But the reliability of the latest BMW engine was lamentable, and at Zolder the team broke five examples in qualifying alone.

After six straight DNFs, in Canada Nelson put the BT53 on pole and led from start to finish. Perversely, it was one of the few occasions since he had wrestled with the BS Fabs McLaren M23 at Zandvoort in 1978 that he wished the car would blow up. He started the race weakened by mild food poisoning, then quickly discovered that his right foot was being cooked. A new front-mounted oil radiator generated so much heat that the brake pedal became almost red hot.

'We could hear him yelling with pain into his helmet over the radio intercom,' reported a crew member. With his pal Niki Lauda chasing him, Nelson found enough reasons to dig into the resources of will and determination which he knows he can rely on when the occasion demands. He got a special round of applause as he hobbled onto the top step of the podium.

One week later, in Detroit, he was back on the top step. This time he was suffering from a crick in the neck, the consequence of a multiple startline accident which

destroyed his race car and forced him to take the spare. But Detroit was to be Nelson's last win of the season. He should have won the Austrian GP, where he and his crew failed to notice in the closing stages that a serious gearbox problem was slowing Lauda's McLaren. As a crew member said, however, 'when your engine is as fragile as the BMW was at that time, you're happy to finish second' – which Nelson did.

Lauda took the championship in the final race, at Estoril, by finishing second to Prost and squeaking home by half a point. Interviewed the following morning, Nelson did not hide his admiration for the McLaren team's achievement in winning 12 of the 16 races. At the same time, he issued a prophetic warning of what can go wrong in a team without a designated number one driver.

'Inside the team, unless you have a driver who will help his team-mate to win points, or always stay behind him, it can screw up all the championship. McLaren was lucky, because nobody could beat their cars this year: for example, in all the races when I was leading them, I broke down. But if I had been in the championship with a chance, and if Gordon hadn't stopped development on this car, it could have been a different story for McLaren.'

The reason Murray had 'stopped development' was that Brabham and BMW were preparing for their new alliance with Pirelli in 1985. The Italian tyre company had been in F1 with Toleman since 1981, and had supplied many of the minor teams. Now, the objective was to beat Goodyear. To do so required an alliance with a major team.

Hindsight now suggests that Brabham was the wrong team for Pirelli to have chosen. Even setting aside its unreliability, the BMW engine was already beginning to be outclassed.

As with all his team's new projects, Nelson threw his weight behind the Pirelli initiative. Intensive testing, including two mammoth winter sessions in South Africa, found him doing the lion's share of the work, since Ecclestone had allowed his team-mate Teo Fabi to join Toleman, and a number two driver was not recruited until shortly before the season started, when the lanky French no-hoper François Hesnault was taken on.

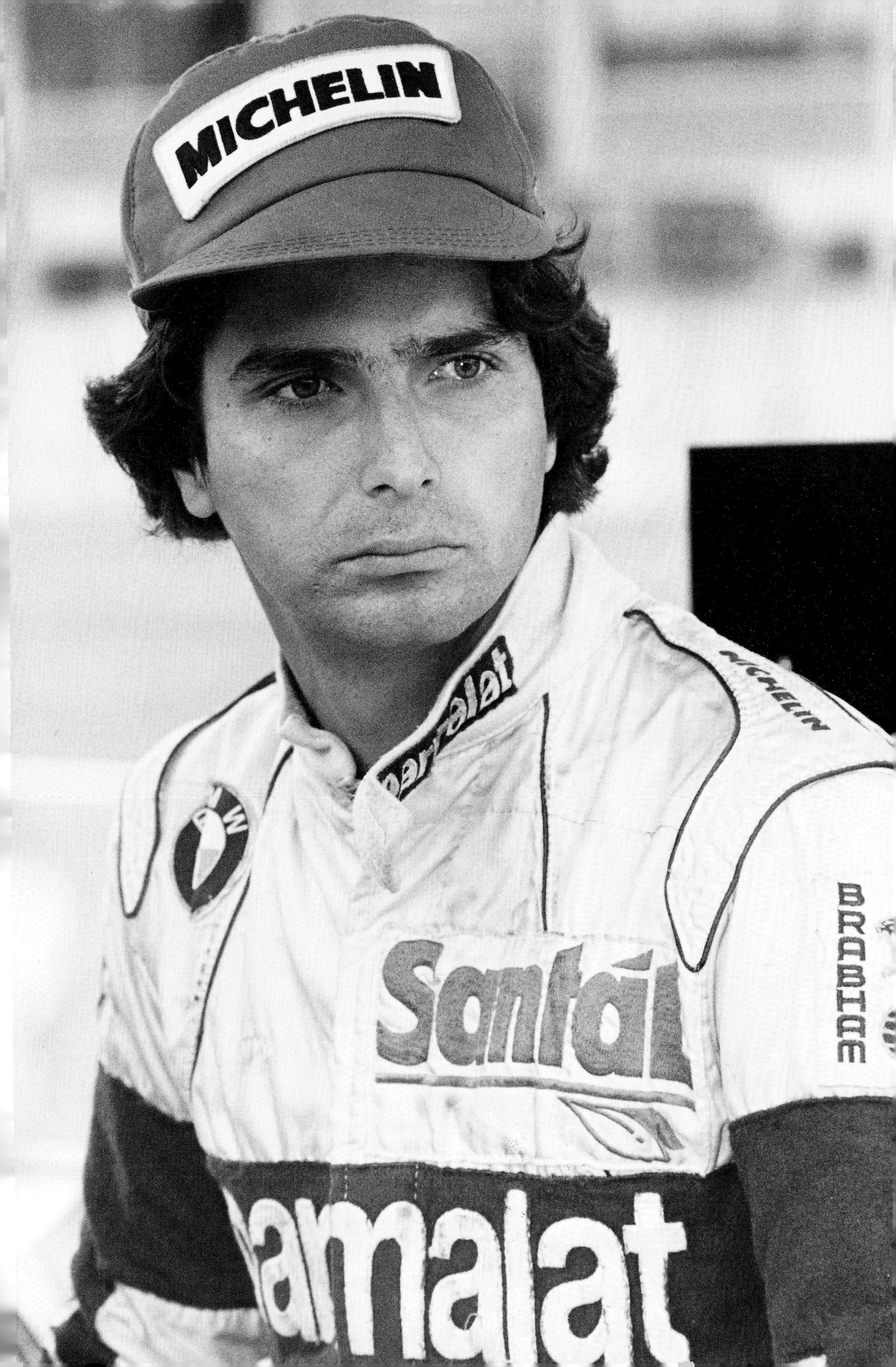
MICHELIN
MICHELIN
BRABHAM
Santal
amalat

Nelson was impressed by Pirelli's dedication. 'They did not start seriously in F1 until the beginning of 1985. They had been running for two or three years before that, but the tyres they had then were ridiculous. Very quickly, they changed all the construction: in South Africa, every two days we received new tyres, modified already from the information we had just got. Then we'd test them to see if they were good enough. And they seemed to make a lot of progress.'

Pirelli got its reward at Ricard, where Nelson was able to exploit one of its harder compounds. In sweltering heat, the Brabham-BMW had visibly superior traction to the Williams-Honda of Keke Rosberg, who was beaten into second place.

Nelson, though, was thinking about a change of scenery. He was still smarting from the Brazilian GP, in which Bernie Ecclestone had accused him of making a driving mistake which put the Brabham off the road on the third lap. When it was retrieved, the mechanics established that the cause of the accident was a broken differential.

Perhaps Nelson, like Fangio in the Fifties, somehow anticipated the difficulties that Brabham was about to face and its demise as a true top team. The Pirelli deal had presented Nelson with a challenge that he had enjoyed, but while the team concentrated on developing its new tyres other aspects had suffered. 'The result', said Nelson, 'was that we improved the car from last year maybe ten per cent, but everybody else improved much more. That was the thing: we got left behind.'

Williams, by contrast, was making lots of progress with Honda. But the team was about to lose Keke Rosberg to McLaren. And Honda – whose fortunes were then inextricably linked with Williams – needed a driver to replace him who had lots of turbo experience. Piquet fitted the bill. He had a number of discussions with Frank Williams, and the two of them finally signed a two-year deal, with $3.3 million for 1986 alone, in Frank's loaned Rover 3500 on the evening before the Austrian GP.

Nelson had hidden none of this from Bernie Ecclestone, but his boss had refused to believe that Frank Williams was willing, or able, to pay the sort of money that would take his driver away. He could not accept that Piquet would leave a team that had become, in his own words, 'my family'. In making the decision to join Williams, Nelson certainly found his loyalties divided. 'After seven years with Brabham it would be easy for me to say that I'm leaving because I want a change, that I want to start all over again,' he remarked. 'But that's not true. I wanted to stay with Brabham, it's *my* team, and I belong there.

'Maybe I made this move to Williams because I wanted to screw Bernie. Because he's so clever, for the last seven years he's been able to screw me in deals and in other ways. Now I want people to see he's not so clever. And he let go me, so now he's in the shit with the sponsors, in the shit with Pirelli and in the shit with everybody, because he's got no good drivers to put in his cars.'

At the time Nelson had to explain to himself why he had left Brabham. 'Maybe I did this because, as I now realise, I wanted to prove that with the new team I have a potential which is perhaps even much stronger than Brabham,' he said. 'If I win the championship here [at Brabham] next year, or in two years, then it will have been pure luck. I didn't want to go to Williams, because I'm very happy here. I didn't want to try a new thing, because I was afraid.

*Winning a scooter for each of his nine pole positions in
1984, Nelson got plenty of opportunities to meet
Piaggio's personality girl Emanuela Enfi. They were
an item off-track, too, throughout 1984 and '85.*

'Now I'm not afraid any more, I'm very enthusiastic, I want to get on with it. If only
Bernie would release me, then I would go testing with Frank immediately, all the time.
Brabham was comfortable, yes: the same mechanics, the same people, it's been like a
family. Everybody knows me, they do what I say. It may not be like that with Frank,
not until time passes and they know me and start to believe in me.'

Eventually he rationalised the decision on purely financial grounds. 'The truth is that
I moved to a similar team with the same potential to make much more money. I told
Bernie that I worked hard for him, so why couldn't I make the same money that Niki
and Prost and everybody was making? Either from principle or because he didn't want
to, Bernie would not pay me. He didn't care. But I didn't want to get involved in some
sort of commercial [bargaining]. I'm not that kind of person.

'Bernie was very disappointed, because he likes to make a bargain [and split] the dif-
ference. But I didn't want to play like this. I was honest with him, and he didn't seem
to care. That is the truth.'

The reward for F3 success came in August: Nelson
tackled his first World Championship round at the
wheel of the works Ensign-Ford in the 1978 German
GP at Hockenheim.

Right: *Still in only his third season of F1, Nelson took three victories with the Brabham BT49-Ford in 1980 but was destined to lose the title in a clash with arch-rival Alan Jones.*

Making plans for the future: at Silverstone in 1981 (below) Nelson discusses prospects for the BMW turbo-powered Brabham BT50 with BMW's Dieter Stappert (with glasses) and chassis wizard Gordon Murray.

Right: *Starting from pole, Nelson should have won the 1984 Austrian GP. After a heart-stopping slide, though, he ceded the lead to Niki Lauda's McLaren-TAG (in fourth place here) and drove cautiously to finish second. In this pre-radio communications era, though, he did not discover until too late that Lauda was in serious gearbox trouble for the last half-dozen laps.*

Right: *On a sizzling afternoon at Ricard in July 1985, Pirelli's race tyres had a decisive advantage, allowing Nelson to give the Milanese company its first GP success since Stirling Moss's Vanwall victory at Monza in 1957.*

*Previous spread: Although he won his first race for the
Williams-Honda team, Nelson was never as
comfortable there as he had been with Brabham.
Nevertheless, Hungary was a satisfying victory for
him as he took advantage of a special differential to
defeat Ayrton Senna and to lap his own team-mate
Nigel Mansell.*

*The 1987 World Championship was Nelson's reward
for three wins and no fewer than seven second places, the
last of them (below) in Mexico. This race was won by
his Williams-Honda 'partner' Nigel Mansell, who was
destined to crash out of contention for the title during
qualifying for the following race, in Japan.*

*Rarely spotted without a lovely girl at his side, Nelson
is seen here with Catherine Valentin, the Belgian
fashion model who presented him with his third son,
Laszlo, in 1988.*

*Right: Of Williams, Nelson said: 'I always intended
to spend the rest of my career with this team.' Due to
misunderstandings and disagreements, the alliance
lasted only two seasons, although it brought him his
third title, in 1987.*

Left: *Victory in the 1987 Hungarian GP was Nelson's only after Mansell lost a wheel nut and retired with four laps to go while leading. Afterwards, the Williams crew discovered that Nelson's car had also been about to lose a nut…*

Despite almost incessant testing, the Lotus 100T was no match for the all-conquering McLarens with their identical Honda V6 turbo engines. Later studies indicated that the yellow car's suspension and chassis were cursed with too much 'flex'.

Overleaf: *Those who still believed that Nelson had 'lucked' into a drive with Benetton-Ford for 1990 attributed his Suzuka win to the errors committed by rivals. They were dumbfounded, though, when he doubled up with a fighting victory in Adelaide at the expense of a desperately late-braking Nigel Mansell.*

*Almost 20 years after they had met in Brasilia, Nelson
was reunited with his friend Roberto Moreno, who took
over the injured Alessandro Nannini's Benetton at
Suzuka in 1990 and promptly finished second behind
the man he described as being 'like a brother'.*

*Even when he is not in the public eye, Nelson is usually
the centre of female attention.*

When Nelson signed with Frank Williams in August 1985, there was not a cloud in his sky. He was contracted as the team's number one driver, and his team-mate – like Riccardo Patrese before – was evidently no threat. An Englishman with five seasons of worthy but uninspiring experience behind him, his best results in GPs had been a few third places with Lotus. Anyone could see that Nelson's new number two was no threat. His name was Nigel Mansell.

Nelson buckled down willingly to winter testing. He did a good job and the team arrived in Brazil for the first race with a well set-up car and probably the most powerful engine on the grid. Mansell saw the race as an opportunity to show his new team-mate who was the real number one. In a scuffle with Ayrton Senna, the Englishman promptly spun off. Nelson Piquet won the Brazilian GP for the second time, and no one could argue that he was the favourite for the 1986 world title.

But a couple of things had changed at Williams. For one, Frank Williams himself was confined to a wheelchair, victim of a road accident. For another, Nigel Mansell had won two races at the end of 1985 and had blossomed as a real challenger. For yet another, Williams's second race engineer had been fired, and for most of the races his place as Mansell's engineer would be taken by Patrick Head, the most senior man at Williams after Frank himself.

*Posing for publicity shots with team chief Frank
Williams; the smiles on his drivers' faces look rather less
than sincere…*

All these things piled up in Nelson's mind. Although he was working well, he had
not established the same closeness with the Williams crew that he had at Brabham. In
other words, he was not comfortable. When his car finished a race, he was usually in
the points, but there were three retirements in the first eight rounds. Going to the
British GP, Mansell had won three times and stood only one point behind World
Championship leader Alain Prost. Nelson trailed his team-mate by 15 points.

At Brands Hatch, Mansell was on a roll. He had won his first GP there only nine
months earlier, and he was again inspired by the adoring crowd. Nelson was confident
he could meet the challenge, and when Mansell's car broke its transmission going to
the first corner victory for Piquet looked certain. However, the race was halted by an
accident involving Jacques Laffite, and Mansell got a second chance, ironically using
Piquet's spare car which the Englishman had not touched all weekend.

The Williams duo were soon into the lead, Piquet-Mansell, after the restart. But
when Nelson missed a gear on lap 23, Mansell did not hesitate to take advantage. 'I
could have closed the door on him, but at the speed he was going he would have taken
us both out of the race,' said Piquet. Soon after he had made a planned tyre stop, however, Nelson received no such courtesy from Mansell, whose tyres were not yet up to
temperature after his own scheduled stop. Mansell held ground and won the race.

Opposite: *First race with Williams-Honda, first
victory: with his arm around the spoils, Nelson's future
at Williams looked assured.*

Beaten by Mansell and Prost at Montreal in 1986,
Nelson never revealed that his chances had been wrecked
by a grabbing rear brake pad.

Nelson had just been exposed to an experience that he had never had before, but one which would be repeated rather frequently in the next 18 months. He had been vanquished by a team-mate of near-equal ability who was prepared to take greater risks and who refused to move over.

Nelson's policy of finishing races at all costs was unchanged but, on the day, it was Mansell on the top step of the podium. The British papers in particular turned on Piquet as 'uninspired' and 'unconvincing'. This was uncomfortable for a man with two World Championships behind him: he was convinced, and remains so, that Mansell should have understood that his 'number two' status barred him from overtaking the team's nominated leader. To Nelson, the team's objective was to win the championship, and by allowing Mansell to beat him that objective was compromised. The results of the 1986 World Championship would, of course, prove Nelson correct.

If he had been a more assiduous reader of newspapers and magazines, Nelson would surely have better understood Frank Williams's definition of what constituted a 'number one' driver. In the rain-soaked 1981 Brazilian GP, Williams drivers Alan Jones and Carlos Reutemann had dominated the race. Although he had been in second place after the start, Jones, the designated 'number one', had expected Reutemann to move over for him, and pit signals had been shown to the Argentine. He had ignored them, an unsurprising decision so close to his home, and Frank Williams had sworn never to let himself be humiliated in front of the world again by a disobedient driver.

Later Nelson admitted that 'the big mistake I made with Frank Williams was not to

write down everything we agreed. Frank was a very trustable guy that I knew for many years.' It would have been possible, of course, for the employee to knock on his boss's door to get the whole thing settled – but he never did. 'I didn't go to Williams to compete with another driver,' he says. 'I had a number one contract, and they screwed up the whole thing by doing what they've done.

'I didn't make a big argument in 1986 only because of [the road accident] that happened to Frank. If I had been obliged to fight with Nigel in Brazil already, and Frank had been there, I would have said, "What the hell am I doing here? You pay me a lot of money, to come here and fight another driver in the same team? And then at the end of the year to risk losing the championship?"

'But I didn't have Frank there, and the situation was very difficult. I felt that I couldn't go to the hospital and say, "Hey, Frank, look: the situation is like this, etc." I shut up and waited to see how things were going. And what happened in 1986 was that we lost the championship: not only me, but also Nigel lost the championship. And they [Williams and Head] didn't learn the lesson...'

To beat Mansell, Nelson could have adopted the braggadocio Mansell style, taken risks and possibly jeopardised his car's reliability. Instead, he withdrew into himself and entered into a phase of psychological warfare against Mansell. At Hockenheim he had a stroke of luck when he made an unscheduled early stop for tyres, and was sent back into the race with a set that had been prepared for Mansell, who had reported deteriorated handling (caused by a collapsed undertray).

Nelson won that one, and at the new Hungaroring he was again on top of the podium following a memorable struggle with Ayrton Senna's Lotus-Renault. In testing, he had discovered a differential which gave a worthwhile performance advantage on slow corners. Nelson insists that Mansell had also tested the diff but had failed to appreciate its advantages. Somehow, he and his engineer Frank Dernie had managed to keep their discovery a secret from Mansell, and when Nelson opted for the special diff on Sunday it passed without notice – until he lapped Mansell.

Both Williams drivers retired at the Österreichring, but at Monza Nelson took his third win in four races. A minor change to his rear wing settings before the start gave a low-downforce set-up which was enough to beat his team-mate again. Though Mansell won magnificently in Portugal, he made a bad start in Mexico and was beaten into fifth place by Nelson.

Going into the final round at Adelaide, both Mansell and Prost in first and second places in the table were having to discard points under the 'best 11 from 16' system. Nelson was back in the reckoning, though he would have to defeat both rivals to become champion. His brother Geraldo, who had been present at both his previous championship-winning GPs, made the journey down under. Given the dominance of the Williams-Honda all season, it was unthinkable that anyone other than a Williams driver should be champion.

Mansell and Piquet filled the first row, and the Englishman was being untypically careful as Piquet and Senna pursued him to the first corner. 'It was fantastic, like three dogs trying to bite a cat,' said Nelson, who came round in front at the end of the first lap. Having let Rosberg through, and trying hard to keep up his lap speeds in spite of

Inset top: *More forced smiles at Adelaide in 1986, the race which Alain Prost (centre) won to become the unexpected champion.*

Main picture: *Early in the race Nelson heads Mansell and eventual winner Prost.*

pessimistic fuel readings, he spun down to fourth, allowing Rosberg and Prost to make it 1–2 for McLaren.

Goodyear had advised everyone to make tyre stops in the race. When Alain Prost cut a tyre and stopped to change all four, a close examination of the Frenchman's undamaged tyres indicated that a non-stop race was in fact possible. If Nigel Mansell had not followed that advice, perhaps his rear tyre would not have exploded and probably he would have been able to defeat Prost.

Less well publicised were the wicked thoughts going through Nelson's head. Moments before Mansell's spectacular exit, Rosberg had retired with a delaminated rear tyre, and suddenly the Williams pit was faced with a dilemma. 'They radioed me to say that Keke had one tyre explode, Nigel had one tyre explode, what did I think about coming in to change the tyres?

'Five laps before, I had started to have some little tyre vibrations. When they said there had been two tyres explode, I thought a little bit and worked out that I had nothing to lose, because if I stopped I was going to finish third in the championship anyway, so I'd better continue. But in another place the vibration started to get worse and worse, and I decided to come in and change tyres and hope that something would happen to Prost.'

It did not, and Prost sailed home to wins in the race and the championship. Nelson congratulated him and McLaren on doing a better job than his own team had done, just as Alain had congratulated him at Kyalami in '83.

Did the decision to stop for tyres cost Nelson and Williams the 1986 championship? 'You never know,' he says. 'Maybe I'd have stuck it in the wall.' Then the malicious look comes across his face. 'You know, the best situation in Australia that time would have been Prost in front, Keke second, me third and Nigel fourth. Nigel just needed third place to be champion, so I could have called the pits by radio and said, "Hey, get on to Nigel and ask him how much he will pay to let him pass. Tell him it's $250,000 for him to win the championship." I would have negotiated for sure. And if he had agreed, I would probably have changed my mind.'

Such was the atmosphere at Williams going into 1987. Hoping that Frank Williams had learned from the first season that it can be counter-productive to allow two drivers in the same team to fight it out, Nelson started his second season at Williams apprehensively. He had been identified by most of the British press as a cry-baby who couldn't take a thrashing from the noble Mansell.

Nelson articulated his philosophy again. 'I am in racing to win the championship, not to fight with another driver in the same team, not to show him I am better. I have nothing to prove. I won already two championships. What I want now is to win more races and more championships. I don't want to compare myself with Nigel or Alain. I want to take my experience, which I got through so many years, not to teach someone how to set up his car and let him make it difficult for me to win races.'

Selfish though it may sound, it was exactly this approach which would ultimately win him the 1987 World Championship.

Through the winter of 1986/87, Nelson worked on the active-ride suspension being developed by Williams. Mansell, who had had a few frights with the Lotus 'active' project in 1983, did not want to be involved. Nelson says Mansell behaved just as Patrese had done over the BMW engine at Brabham in 1982. 'Nigel tried it a couple of times,' claims Nelson, 'but then he refused to have anything to do with it. The team came to me and said, "Look, do you want to have the project?"

'I said, "OK, I will take on the whole project. But if it's good, I want you to promise that I get it only for me." Why should I go balls out every day, taking risks just so that Nigel can have it too? I even suggested that we share the programme. But he [Mansell] said, "No, I'm not interested, the thing won't work." I was happy to do all the work, though, because I knew the potential of the active ride.'

Although it was destined to be crucial to Nelson's hopes, the new suspension would have to wait until later in the season. In Brazil, Nelson lost to Prost due to overheating, caused by paper in the radiator intakes. In qualifying for the next race, at Imola, he came close to losing his life.

It was Friday afternoon and Nelson had just set the fastest time of the session. At the 190 mph Tamburello swerve, his car got out of shape and slammed sideways into the retaining wall. There were anxious moments as the driver, unconscious for several minutes, was removed from the wreck. A quick helicopter flight took him to hospital in Bologna, where he was held overnight. Marks on the track suggested a tyre failure, and Goodyear called for reserves of a different type of tyre to be brought in quickly.

When Nelson returned on Saturday morning, he wanted to get back into the spare Williams. There followed an animated discussion with Professor Syd Watkins, FISA's medical expert, who had to point out that, however ready Nelson might be to drive again, it was a risk that he could not approve. Despite a painfully twisted foot and other abrasions, Nelson tried to insist. Finally, the matter was resolved when Williams withdrew the entry.

With a miserable Piquet in the TV Globo box, Mansell handily won the race on Sunday. Although Nelson led the Spa race two weeks later until an engine problem stopped him, at Monaco he had to admit that he was still handicapped by the foot injury and his lack of physical fitness. Indeed, the Imola bang had knocked the stuffing out of the Brazilian, who confessed to being unable to sleep or even concentrate on reading a magazine. It was only when he got some specialist treatment that matters improved.

Still, he wanted to downplay what had happened. 'You need a big shunt like Pironi's, something that puts you in hospital for a long time and really hurts you, to make you think hard,' he said. 'Until this moment, I never had anything as bad as that.'

With his team-mate recovering, Nigel Mansell hit terrific form. But although Mansell scored scintillating victories at Paul Ricard and Silverstone, in the four races after Spa Nelson collected more points by finishing four times in second place. Preoccupied though he was with finishing, Nelson had set his heart on defeating Mansell 'at home', an aim which went badly wrong.

Most British fans will remember that afternoon for a lifetime. Not many of them, though, will know what a gamble their 'True Brit' hero was taking with his fuel allocation.

For Nelson, Silverstone was a disappointment but not a disaster. A setback for

A clean start at Rio put Nelson in front of arch-rival Senna in the 1987 Brazilian GP. Paper debris in the radiator ducts of the Williams-Honda caused overheating which allowed Alain Prost (1) to come through and win.

90

Yet another second place: Detroit 1987 was just one of
the seven races in which Nelson racked up six points on
the way to becoming champion for the third time.

Mansell turned into an unexpected bonus after he stopped to change an unbalanced tyre, and the fresh set proved to be perfect for fast laps. It was the tension which built up as Mansell chased Nelson for the lead, then sold him a spectacular 'dummy' at Stowe with barely three laps to go, which made the race special.

The Williams team has since revealed that Mansell's onboard fuel read-out, normally accurate to within a few hundred yards, showed that he should never have finished the race. 'My fuel had been well behind on the meter, but I was able to bring it back and back,' says Nelson. 'I was still behind, so when I saw Nigel coming from behind and the times he was doing, I said, "Jeez, how does he do it?" It was unbelievable to me, because he always used much more fuel than me, and he was coming very quick.

'To cut things short, he took a gamble. According to his meter, his fuel [should have] finished one lap before the finish. But he continued going, and he finished the race. Of course, it was the right thing to do. I was running on the fuel meter. I had one and a half litres left in the tank, and I could have gone a little bit quicker. There was some trouble from me for the Honda people after that, though...'

Mansell himself has since conceded that he had no intention of being beaten in 'his' race, and that his engine blew up on the slowing-down lap when the fuel ran out and the hot pistons seized. Nelson may have left Silverstone with the jeers of the crowd echoing in his ears, but he had 30 points in the bank, exactly the same as Mansell, and now they were only one point behind Ayrton Senna.

Victories in three of the next four races, two of them at the expense of the luckless Mansell, gave Nelson a 14-point lead in the championship. The most satisfying of them was certainly at Monza, where he was allowed to bring out the 'active' car for its maiden appearance. He passed Senna's Lotus-Honda as it ran wide on worn tyres, and held off the Lotus driver's comeback: Mansell's car overheated and he finished third.

In Hungary, Camel had announced that Nelson would be joining Lotus for 1988. The fact that he would be replacing Senna was an embarrassment for his fellow-Brazilian, whose widely rumoured switch to McLaren had yet to be announced. Due to extensive flights around Europe, Nelson had to break the news to Frank Williams by sticking a hand-written note under his boss's hotel room door in Budapest.

He had wanted to go because none of Frank Williams's undertakings – real or imagined – about holding back Mansell had been kept. 'The Lotus deal happened very quick. Peter [Warr] contacted me for the first time in Hockenheim. He came to Nice on the Saturday after Hockenheim. I made a proposal to him. He moved very quickly; he went back to England and talked to the sponsors. They wanted to see me, I arrived there [London], we discussed for one afternoon, and I signed next day [Thursday 6 August] at 10 o'clock. I wanted to be a number one driver, in a good team...and I got what I wanted.'

In his delight at upstaging Senna, he tried hard to be magnanimous about Williams. 'I'm sorry that things didn't work the way I wanted. I didn't come to Williams to do only two years, I came to finish my motor racing career, to have a very strong relationship, to race until I was 40 years old, and to win two championships. I'm not the sort of driver who jumps from one team to another one. But it's nothing to do with Frank as a person.'

Spelling it out for the author at Detroit in 1987.

Though no one at Honda was ever so indiscreet as to suggest that face had been lost in Tokyo following the loss of the World Championship in 1986, or even as a result of the Piquet–Mansell feud in 1987, Nelson heard a report to that effect. He appears to have been better informed than Patrick Head, who went to see him at Biggin Hill where Nelson flew in early August for an hour's chat.

'When I heard that if I left Williams there was a chance that they would lose the engine, I told Patrick, "It's OK, I [will] put up with the shit and I stay, because I don't want to be the reason for you losing the engine."

'Patrick talked about this and that, but basically he was saying that Williams had the Honda engine for sure in 1988, it was not important what I did. So I straight off went to talk to the other people.' One month after the news of Nelson's Lotus deal had been released in Hungary, Honda offered its 'thanks' to Williams for its help...and announced that it would be supplying Lotus and McLaren in 1988.

Less knowledgeable about Lotus than he had been about Honda, Nelson offered his opinion that Ayrton Senna had 'not been experienced enough' to sort out the Lotus-Honda in 1987. This and some unreported remarks about his private life infuriated Senna so much that before the end of the year there was a fresh feud brewing between Nelson and a fellow driver.

As we have seen, Nelson reads nothing about racing, which makes it difficult for him to imagine the impact of the written word on those who do. It was around the time of his move to Lotus that he had taken up with Catherine Valentin, the Belgian model who was to become his 'official consort' and bear him a child, a third son, Laszlo, in 1988. It has been speculated that much of Nelson's information about Senna's habits came from Miss Valentin, who had been seen briefly on Senna's arm in 1987.

Eduardo Prado recalls Senna's fury, which had built up to a peak immediately after the Portuguese GP. 'I had arrived in Lisbon after the race, to be with Nelson at Jerez one week later,' he recalls. 'Ayrton passed a message to two of Nelson's friends. He was really mad, his eyes were red, and they got very worried when Ayrton said, "Look, tell this son of a bitch of a friend of yours that I'm going to kill him."'

Nelson calmly dismissed the threat and forgot it. He has never taken the 'feud' with Senna as seriously as the press, and is unaware of the fact that the little 'digs' at his fellow-countryman always get back to him and irritate him mightily.

In Brazil, many believe that Senna hates Piquet because of an alleged attempt in 1983 to keep Senna from joining Brabham. Eduardo Prado, though, sees it differently.

'I was in England that summer, and Nelson called me one night to ask if I knew about some guy he had met at the Brabham factory, a Brazilian who was winning lots of F3 races. I said, "Yes, his name is Ayrton Senna and he looks as though he's going to be champion. Why?"

'Nelson said, "Oh, he's been to see Bernie today about getting a Formula 1 drive. But Bernie's crazy. He said he wants him to sign for five years, and to pay nothing for the first two years." Senna was thinking about paying Toleman for a place there, but Nelson had suggested taking the number two position at Brabham because it was a much better team.

'Nelson actually recommended Senna to join his team. "I have been here for quite a

while," he told Senna. "I've already been World Champion, and probably I will move on one day. You could become number one driver here, like I did when Niki left." Nelson didn't seem impressed, he didn't know who the guy was.'

The 1987 title was Nelson's two days before the Japanese GP, when Mansell's car spun during qualifying, hit a tyre wall and rode up in the air before crashing down on a kerb. Its driver, who has always maintained that something went wrong with the car, was on the plane back to London that night.

Not surprisingly, Nelson believes that Mansell was simply trying too hard. His theory that World Championships can be won by caution rather than outright speed was vindicated. But he would not finish either of his final two races with Williams, and his departure had an unpleasant, sour note to it.

'Everyone was saying I won the championship because Nigel did not race in Japan,' he explains. 'That was not true: I won because I was 15 effing points in front of him. Of course, it's much better to win the race and win the championship at the same time. It's quite true I had a not very good year, with being affected very much from the accident I had in Imola. Last year he was 50 per cent of the times quicker than me, I was 50 per cent quicker than him. But in the races I was 90 per cent quicker than him; I did eight fastest laps,'

When someone mentioned that Alain Prost had stated that it had been a lucky win, Nelson erupted. 'It's not true!' he reacted. 'Alain was lucky last year that we fought each other and Nigel blew his tyre in Adelaide. That was Alain being lucky. This year, being 15 points in front of Nigel was not luck, I was champion by being consistent and by finishing all the races. That's the deal. The name of the game is to win by getting more points, not by winning. In some of the races I finished second on purpose because I needed the six points in the hand more...I didn't know for sure that I could get the nine points.'

One day, perhaps, Frank Williams will be willing to tell the team's side of the missed opportunities and personality disaffections inside his team. But he has declined to go over this period with the author. Nelson's departure coincided with Honda's, and Williams went into a period of decline.

Nevertheless, Nelson enjoyed certain aspects of the two years with Williams. He is still friendly with Patrick Head, to whom he became closer in the second year, when he was no longer engineering Mansell's car. 'I enjoyed collaborating with him,' says Piquet, 'he is a very honest person who always says what he thinks.' Frank, too, has fond memories of Nelson now. Soon after the break-up, Nelson found a special telephone designed for handicapped people. He sent it to Frank, whose business life has been transformed by being able to receive and dial calls without help.

Nelson's two years at Lotus were much less fruitful. Even before the first race, they began badly when, first, a Brazilian reporter headlined an off-hand comment which Nelson had made about Senna, and then, soon after, *Playboy* (Brazil) published an interview with Nelson.

The newspaper comment, which seemed innocuous enough, led to a legal process which was only recently settled out of court. The *Playboy* interview, with Nelson being outrageously honest on several topics, would also haunt him for months.

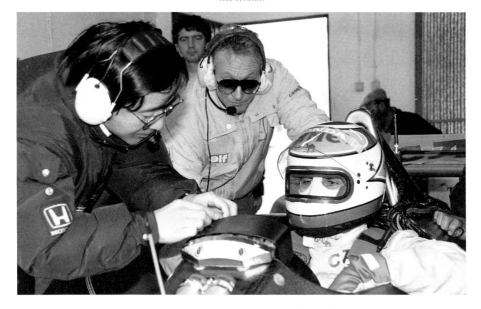

*Always a fan of Honda, Nelson chats with engineer
Goto. By the end of the 1988 season, his relations with
Lotus designer Gérard Ducarouge (rear) were much
less cordial.*

Perhaps the most controversial comments concerned the future of Ferrari after the
death of Enzo Ferrari, whose health was in a slow but irreversible decline.

Virtually everything Nelson forecast was to come true. But although his comments
made him exceedingly unpopular, he still does not regret them. 'If it was not for my
sponsors, this thing would not have happened, because I don't give interviews. I didn't
lie. I didn't say anything horrible. Everything came true...not just about Ferrari but
everything else I said was true.'

But the British press picked up on some remarks about Mansell's family. While Nelson should never have made such personal observations, it was surely hypocritical of
Fleet Street to hurt Mansell by translating them (somewhat inaccurately) and then publishing them in English. Nelson claims that Mansell brushed aside his attempts to
apologise, and agrees that he should not have answered questions on such matters. But
it remains astonishing that newspapermen, always so hungry for an off-the-cuff quote
from a sportsman, should have condemned him for being so frank.

Senior officials of Camel, Lotus's sponsor, bit their lips about their new driver's
indiscretions. But it was at the second race of the season, Imola, that Honda told Lotus
manager Peter Warr that there would be no engines for the team in 1989. Although
everyone was being very guarded in their comments, it was obvious that the Lotus-
Honda designed by Gérard Ducarouge had some major faults. It was no match for the
McLaren with its identical turbo V6 and, although it finished third both in Brazil and
at Imola, it was sometimes inferior to the normally aspirated cars.

The mediocre performance of the 100T came as a terrible shock to Nelson, who had
started his Lotus period with innate confidence in Ducarouge. Much later it would be
revealed by the team that the car lacked torsional rigidity, both in its chassis and in its
suspension uprights. In thousands of kilometres of testing it would not respond to
adjustments, and the project would result in Ducarouge's departure.

Nelson was bitter, so vindictive in the end that it is better not to publish some of his comments about the Frenchman. By the end of the year, Lotus had recruited Frank Dernie, Nelson's former engineer at Williams. But although Dernie developed a small, compact car around a 'customer' Judd engine, the V8 lacked both power and reliability against the V10 and V12 units introduced for the return to naturally aspirated engines in 1989.

A rib-cracking accident on board his new boat left Nelson in acute pain at the beginning of the new season. It also focused unwelcome attention on the wealth that he was accumulating thanks to the $6.5 million annual retainer which he had negotiated with Camel.

The boat, a 35-metre motor yacht which had been named the *Pilar Rossi* in honour of his old friend Ronnie Rossi's fashion-designer wife, was built in Turkey and fitted out in Italy. With its three staterooms and a heli-pad on the rear for Nelson's new Hughes chopper, it was flashy even by Monégasque standards. Ironically, Nelson was now officially resident in Malta, although the boat is moored off Monaco most of the time.

By mid-1989, Nelson had been written off by many pressmen as a serious force in F1. Setting aside tyre affiliations, though, he was competitive with other V8 cars, and he maintained that he was still trying as hard as ever. He insisted that he was driving to the limits of the Lotus, and beyond. Controversial as ever, he claimed that he was giving better value for money than Alain Prost, who would be World Champion that year.

'I still risk like crazy, because I like motor racing. The day I cannot take risks any more, that's the day when I'll say [that] I have to stop. But I don't think Prost could say the same thing. He claims it's not important to push hard in qualifying, but it *is* important. He knows it's important, maybe he cannot do it [any more]. At Monaco, where he gave up, he said, "Oh, it's not important, etc." Bullshit! It's important, that's why everybody fights like crazy.'

When he failed to qualify for the 1989 Belgian GP at Spa, Nelson himself came in for suggestions that he didn't try hard enough. His team-mate Nakajima had also failed to get in, and inevitably the denizens of the press room clucked disapprovingly. Team Lotus had never before failed to get a car onto the grid, and there was talk of how badly the historic team had been let down.

Reality was rather different. Friday's qualifying had been wet, and was therefore a write-off for everyone. Having selected two sets of qualifying tyres, each good for only one quick lap of the long Spa-Francorchamps circuit, on Saturday Nelson lost his first chance due to an engine problem. On the second set he had no option but to 'go for it', and he had the misfortune to find Grouillard's Ligier in the way at the fast Pouhon left-hander. On the ragged edge, he was unexpectedly forced off-line…and slithered into the dirt. Not for the first time, the critics who lambasted him for 'not trying hard enough' paradoxically chose to haul him over the coals for having committed himself to what was clearly a ten-tenths effort.

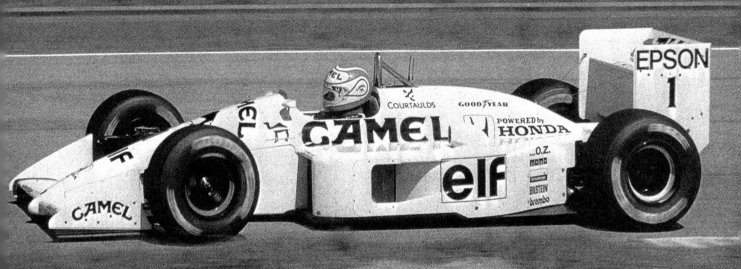

With three miserable fourth places to his credit, and with the Camel people beginning to talk openly of having been deceived, Nelson Piquet was not much in demand for 1990. One of the last seats to be filled by the leading teams was the place alongside Alessandro Nannini at Benetton, where Emanuele Pirro had been disappointing.

Nelson had several allies at Benetton, among them Ford racing supremo Mike Kranefuss, who had tried to tempt him away from Brabham in 1982 to a Ford-backed F1 project which never came to fruition. Kranefuss was not forgiven for favouring Nelson, as he recalls. 'Certain people, specifically a section of the English media, thought they should really let me have it and say, "I don't think that that is such a good decision." But you can only go by your feelings, and the way I talked to Nelson, I honestly felt that he did not want to leave Formula 1 on the note that he was going with Lotus last year. I was totally convinced that, if he was given the right equipment, he would be as good as ever.'

Whatever the media's doubts, most of their interest after Nelson's recruitment by Benetton centred on rumours that he was to get a 'payment by results' deal of a comparatively small retainer coupled with a bonus of $100,000 per point.

Throughout the 1990 season, Nelson mischievously told different stories about the amount of the bonus. His largest hint suggested a mere $12,000. Sources in the team spoke guardedly of a 'seven figure' retainer and a 'six figure' bonus. Given Nelson's own deliberate obstruction and the team's unwillingness to release full details of the contract, the matter remains a mystery. Nevertheless, it did no harm at all to Benetton when TV commentators started to get excited at describing on-screen battles which could make Nelson richer by hundreds of thousands if he was prepared to outbrake a rival.

And there were to be many such battles, for although the Benetton team did not introduce its new car until Imola, and took a little while to refine it, the car had lots of potential, albeit without Honda-beating power from its V8 Ford HB engine. Nelson monotonously racked up points from the very beginning. Paradoxically, his only non-finish came at his unfavourite circuit, Monaco, when he tried a bit too hard to overtake Boutsen, spun and was disqualified.

In the second half of the season there was a hint of things to come when Nannini led the German GP, exploiting the low-downforce set-up of the little car and only yielding to pressure from Senna after leading for 15 laps. Nelson, who had qualified in front of his team-mate, retired with electrical trouble, a gremlin which would repeat itself after he himself had led very briefly in Spain.

He had forecast that the reliability and increasing competitiveness of the car could add up to a race winner before the end of the year. Victory was to come at Suzuka, where a sequence of unforced errors, starting with the Senna/Prost clash at the start, eliminated the Ferrari and McLaren-Honda teams. Accompanied by his friend Roberto Moreno, who had taken over the place left by the injured Nannini and promptly finished second, Nelson greeted the media in the post-race conference with a jaunty 'remember me?'

Other drivers have been away from the winner's circle for longer. Another World Champion, Jack Brabham, went without a win for five years between 1960 and 1966. But perhaps nobody was less expected to return to prominence. When Nelson rubbed it in with a follow-up victory at Adelaide, though, the critics had to admit that his own faith in his ability to win was justified.

*Two wins at the season's end more than justified
Nelson's inclusion in the Benetton-Ford team. His drive
in Australia (above) silenced the doubters who had
questioned his competitiveness and motivation.*

John Barnard, who had joined Benetton shortly before Nelson did, was more than happy with him as a driver. 'He had spent a couple of years going down at a fairly rapid rate, certainly in people's impression of him,' observed Barnard. 'If he was going to continue, he was either going to have to correct that impression, or we would have known that he was there strictly for the money. And that, as you know, has been nothing like as much this year as he's been used to. Since he was prepared to join us on a totally different scale from what he's been used to, I knew that his motivation was still there.

'If you are three-times World Champion, it is impossible to have fluked it three times. People have fluked it once, but you don't fluke it three times. And that means you've got something which is good. He has good feedback and he enjoys working with the team on the car. It's all worked out reasonably well.'

But for how much longer? Nelson's estimate has always been that, as long as there's a good car available, he will be around until he is 40, maybe longer. In a way, he is trapped by F1, not so much by the money – of which he has plenty – but by having been comfortable in it for so long.

'It is the dream of everybody to drive a Formula 1 car. If I gave up, I would probably relax too much. If I did not have something interesting in my life, I would be...well, not an alcoholic or anything like that, but I would probably get bored and become fat. Today, I never drink, I never took any drugs, I never tried anything. The only thing in my blood is racing and more racing. Tomorrow, if I don't race any more, I think I will try *everything*, to see what it is! If you've never tried it, you don't know what it is. I would like to know.'

It is easy to poke fun at Nelson's extended family and complicated relations with women. But all of the girls who have shared their lives with him say that he was, and remains, their friend. Three of them have borne his children and, although he says he will never be a *good* father, he enjoys paternity and being a family man.

'Maybe I will do something good with my life one day,' he once said. 'We are such bloody funny people, we human beings. We try to do good things so that we look good to other people.' He paused, thinking about his project to look after abandoned Brazilian children. For the time being, he can do nothing because in Brazil private orphanages are forbidden by law.

'Now, I get money from rich people that I know. And my mother goes to some of these kids' places for one or two days and writes down everything they need...a new cooker, new beds, new clothes. Then she buys everything herself and delivers it, to make sure it is being used correctly. Then she goes somewhere else.

'Some people in the north of the country heard what she was doing, in one of the cities where my father came from, and they wrote a letter. So my mother went there

and said, "Good, we will start here, we are going to buy an old house." It's such a poor place, and what we have there is not an orphanage, it's a crèche where the children can be during the day. That way, their mothers go to work to make some money, so the family can live.'

On the other side of the world, he has no regrets about his own lifestyle. 'We only have one life,' he says, 'so we have to do everything now, when we can. I have always done the best I could do, every day of my life. But I never had a goal in my life to be World Champion; all this came naturally.'

Such a candid summary of a career filled with so much achievement may sound strange coming from a man who says he never looks back. But, while he may not like to look back, Nelson Piquet is coming to a time when, as he has admitted, he will surely have to start doing so because racing cars will no longer be so attractive.

When he does that, he has promised to write his own book. That is something which will be well worth waiting for. For the time being, this profile will have to do.

NELSON PIQUET · CAREER RECORD
(1977–1990)
BY JOHN TAYLOR

1977

Race	Circuit	Date	Entrant	Car	Comment
European F3 Championship Race–Heat 2	Paul Ricard	20/03/77	Scuderia Mirabella MM	March 773-Toyota	accident
ADAC 300 Km Rennen	Nürburgring	27/03/77	Scuderia Mirabella MM	March 773-Toyota	spun off
European F3 Championship Race	Nürburgring	27/03/77	Scuderia Mirabella MM	March 773-Toyota	
European F3 Championship Race–Heat 1	Zandvoort	11/04/77	Scuderia Mirabella MM	March 773-Toyota	collision
European F3 Championship Race–Heat 1	Zolder	24/04/77	Scuderia Mirabella MM	March 773-Toyota	
European F3 Championship Race–Final	Zolder	24/04/77	Scuderia Mirabella MM	March 773-Toyota	
European F3 Championship Race–Heat 1	Österreichring	08/05/77	Scuderia Mirabella MM	March 773-Toyota	
European F3 Championship Race–Heat 2	Österreichring	08/05/77	Scuderia Mirabella MM	March 773-Toyota	
European F3 Championship Race–Aggregate	Österreichring	08/05/77	Scuderia Mirabella MM	March 773-Toyota	
Monaco F3 Grand Prix	Monte Carlo	21/05/77	Scuderia Mirabella MM	Ralt RT1-Toyota	
European F3 Championship Race–Heat 1	Imola	29/05/77	Scuderia Mirabella MM	Ralt RT1-Toyota	
European F3 Championship Race–Final	Imola	29/05/77	Scuderia Mirabella MM	Ralt RT1-Toyota	
European F3 Championship Race–Heat 2	Enna	12/06/77	Scuderia Mirabella MM	Ralt RT1-Toyota	spun off
European F3 Championship Race–Final	Enna	12/06/77	Scuderia Mirabella MM	Ralt RT1-Toyota	
Vandervell F3 Championship Race–Heat 1	Silverstone	15/07/77	Scuderia Mirabella MM	Ralt RT1-Toyota	
Vandervell F3 Championship Race–Final	Silverstone	16/07/77	Scuderia Mirabella MM	Ralt RT1-Toyota	
European F3 Championship Race–Heat 1	Croix-en-Ternois	24/07/77	Scuderia Mirabella MM	Ralt RT1-Toyota	Pole
European F3 Championship Race–Final	Croix-en-Ternois	24/07/77	Scuderia Mirabella MM	Ralt RT1-Toyota	
European F3 Championship Race–Heat 1	Knutstorp	07/08/77	Scuderia Mirabella MM	Ralt RT1-Toyota	
European F3 Championship Race–Final	Knutstorp	07/08/77	Scuderia Mirabella MM	Ralt RT1-Toyota	Fastest lap
Austrian Grand Prix F3 Race	Österreichring	13/08/77	Scuderia Mirabella MM	Ralt RT1-Toyota	
European F3 Championship Race–Heat 1	Kassel-Calden	21/08/77	Scuderia Mirabella MM	Ralt RT1-Toyota	Pole
European F3 Championship Race–Final	Kassel-Calden	21/08/77	Scuderia Mirabella MM	Ralt RT1-Toyota	
European F3 Championship Race–Heat 1	Donington Park	27/08/77	Scuderia Mirabella MM	Ralt RT1-Toyota	Fastest lap
European F3 Championship Race–Final	Donington Park	27/08/77	Scuderia Mirabella MM	Ralt RT1-Toyota	Fastest lap
Vandervell F3 Championship Race	Silverstone	29/08/77	Scuderia Mirabella MM	Ralt RT1-Toyota	Pole
European F3 Championship Race	Jarama	18/09/77	Scuderia Mirabella MM	Ralt RT1-Toyota	Pole
Sachs Trophy F3 Race–Heat 1	Monza	25/09/77	Scuderia Mirabella MM	Ralt RT1-Toyota	
Sachs Trophy F3 Race–Final	Monza	25/09/77	Scuderia Mirabella MM	Ralt RT1-Toyota	accident
European F3 Championship Race–Heat 1	Vallelunga	09/10/77	Scuderia Mirabella MM	Ralt RT1-Toyota	engine/Fastest lap

1978

Race	Circuit	Date	Entrant	Car	Comment
Vandervell F3 Championship Race	Silverstone	05/03/78	Brastemp/Calbros/Arno	Ralt RT1-Toyota	
BP F3 Championship Race	Thruxton	12/03/78	Brastemp/Calbros/Arno	Ralt RT1-Toyota	
Vandervell F3 Championship Race	Silverstone	19/03/78	Brastemp/Calbros/Arno	Ralt RT1-Toyota	
BP F3 Championship Race	Thruxton	27/03/78	Brastemp/Calbros/Arno	Ralt RT1-Toyota	
World Cup International F3 Race	Donington Park	09/04/78	Brastemp/Calbros/Arno	Ralt RT1-Toyota	gearbox
BP F3 Championship Race	Brands Hatch	16/04/78	Brastemp/Calbros/Arno	Ralt RT1-Toyota	
BP F3 Championship Race	Oulton Park	22/04/78	Brastemp/Calbros/Arno	Ralt RT1-Toyota	spun off/Pole
BP F3 Championship Race	Donington Park	30/04/78	Brastemp/Calbros/Arno	Ralt RT1-Toyota	
Vandervell F3 Championship Race	Silverstone	01/05/78	Brastemp/Calbros/Arno	Ralt RT1-Toyota	
Monaco F3 Grand Prix–Heat 2	Monte Carlo	06/05/78	Brastemp/Calbros/Arno	Ralt RT1-Toyota	fuel leak
BP F3 Championship Race	Mallory Park	14/05/78	Brastemp/Calbros/Arno	Ralt RT1-Toyota	Pole/Fastest lap
Vandervell F3 Championship Race	Oulton Park	20/05/78	Brastemp/Calbros/Arno	Ralt RT1-Toyota	Pole/Fastest lap
BP F3 Championship Race	Thruxton	29/05/78	Brastemp/Calbros/Arno	Ralt RT1-Toyota	
BP F3 Championship Race	Brands Hatch	11/06/78	Brastemp/Calbros/Arno	Ralt RT1-Toyota	Pole/Fastest lap
BP F3 Championship Race	Cadwell Park	25/06/78	Brastemp/Calbros/Arno	Ralt RT1-Toyota	Pole
BP F3 Championship Race	Paul Ricard	02/07/78	Brastemp/Calbros/Arno	Ralt RT1-Toyota	Pole
BP F3 Championship Race	Silverstone	09/07/78	Brastemp/Calbros/Arno	Ralt RT1-Toyota	Pole/Fastest lap
BP F3 Championship Race	Brands Hatch	15/07/78	Brastemp/Calbros/Arno	Ralt RT1-Toyota	Pole
BP F3 Championship Race	Donington Park	23/07/78	Brastemp/Calbros/Arno	Ralt RT1-Toyota	Pole/Fastest lap
GERMAN GP	Hockenheim	30/07/78	Team Tissot-Ensign	Ensign N177-Cosworth DFV	engine
AUSTRIAN GP	Österreichring	13/08/78	BS Fabrications	McLaren M23-Cosworth DFV	slid off road
DUTCH GP	Zandvoort	27/08/78	BS Fabrications/Marlboro	McLaren M23-Cosworth DFV	driveshaft
Vandervell F3 Championship Race	Silverstone	28/08/78	Brastemp/Calbros/Arno	Ralt RT1-Toyota	Pole/Fastest lap
ITALIAN GP	Monza	10/09/78	BS Fabrications/Marlboro	McLaren M23-Cosworth DFV	
Vandervell F3 Championship Race	Silverstone	23/09/78	Brastemp/Calbros/Arno	Ralt RT1-Toyota	
BP F3 Championship Race	Snetterton	25/09/78	Brastemp/Calbros/Arno	Ralt RT1-Toyota	Pole/Fastest lap
Vandervell F3 Championship Race	Silverstone	30/09/78	Brastemp/Calbros/Arno	Ralt RT1-Toyota	Pole
CANADIAN GP	Montreal	08/10/78	Parmalat Racing Team	Brabham BT46-Alfa Romeo 115	

Note:
Nelson Piquet arrived in Europe after a successful career in Brazil racing in both karts and Formula Super Vee.

1979

Pos	Race	Circuit	Date	Team	Car	Notes
ret/dns	ARGENTINE GP	Buenos Aires	21/01/79	Parmalat Racing Team	Brabham BT46-Alfa Romeo 115	*accident in first start*
ret	BRAZILIAN GP	Interlagos	04/02/79	Parmalat Racing Team	Brabham BT48-Alfa Romeo 1260	*hit Regazzoni*
7	SOUTH AFRICAN GP	Kyalami	03/03/79	Parmalat Racing Team	Brabham BT48-Alfa Romeo 1260	
8	US GP WEST	Long Beach	08/04/79	Parmalat Racing Team	Brabham BT48-Alfa Romeo 1260	
2	Marlboro-Daily Mail Race of Champions	Brands Hatch	15/04/79	Parmalat Racing Team	Brabham BT48-Alfa Romeo 1260	*Fastest lap*
ret	SPANISH GP	Jarama	29/04/79	Parmalat Racing Team	Brabham BT48-Alfa Romeo 1260	*fuel metering unit*
dns	BMW Procar Race	Zolder	12/05/79	BMW Racing GmbH	BMW M1	*fuel leak*
ret	BELGIAN GP	Zolder	13/05/79	Parmalat Racing Team	Brabham BT48-Alfa Romeo 1260	*engine*
ret	MONACO GP	Monte Carlo	27/05/79	Parmalat Racing Team	Brabham BT48-Alfa Romeo 1260	*driveshaft*
1	Gunnar Nilsson Memorial Trophy Race	Donington Park	03/06/79	BMW Racing GmbH	BMW M1	*Pole/Fastest lap*
1	BMW Procar Race	Dijon	30/06/79	BMW Racing GmbH	BMW M1	
ret	FRENCH GP	Dijon	01/07/79	Parmalat Racing Team	Brabham BT48-Alfa Romeo 1260	*spun off*
2	BMW Procar Race	Silverstone	13/07/79	BMW Racing GmbH	BMW M1	
ret	BRITISH GP	Silverstone	14/07/79	Parmalat Racing Team	Brabham BT48-Alfa Romeo 1260	*spun off*
12/*ret*	GERMAN GP	Hockenheim	29/07/79	Parmalat Racing Team	Brabham BT48-Alfa Romeo 1260	*engine*
ret	AUSTRIAN GP	Österreichring	12/08/79	Parmalat Racing Team	Brabham BT48-Alfa Romeo 1260	*engine*
ret	BMW Procar Race	Zandvoort	25/08/79	BMW Racing GmbH	BMW M1	*collision with Höttinger*
4	DUTCH GP	Zandvoort	26/08/79	Parmalat Racing Team	Brabham BT48-Alfa Romeo 1260	
ret	BMW Procar Race	Monza	08/09/79	BMW Racing GmbH	BMW M1	*spun off/Pole*
ret	ITALIAN GP	Monza	09/09/79	Parmalat Racing Team	Brabham BT48-Alfa Romeo 1260	*collision with Reutemann*
ret	CANADIAN GP	Montreal	30/09/79	Parmalat Racing Team	Brabham BT49-Cosworth DFV	*gearbox*
ret	US GP EAST	Watkins Glen	07/10/79	Parmalat Racing Team	Brabham BT49-Cosworth DFV	*driveshaft/Fastest lap*

1980

Pos	Race	Circuit	Date	Team	Car	Notes
2	ARGENTINE GP	Buenos Aires	13/01/80	Parmalat Racing Team	Brabham BT49-Cosworth DFV	
ret	BRAZILIAN GP	Interlagos	27/01/80	Parmalat Racing Team	Brabham BT49-Cosworth DFV	*suspension–accident*
4	SOUTH AFRICAN GP	Kyalami	01/03/80	Parmalat Racing Team	Brabham BT49-Cosworth DFV	
1	US GP WEST	Long Beach	30/03/80	Parmalat Racing Team	Brabham BT49-Cosworth DFV	*Pole/Fastest lap*
5	BMW Procar Championship Race	Donington Park	26/04/80	BS Fabrications	BMW M1	
ret	BELGIAN GP	Zolder	04/05/80	Parmalat Racing Team	Brabham BT49-Cosworth DFV	*slid into catch-fence*
ret	BMW Procar Championship Race	AVUS	11/05/80	BS Fabrications	BMW M1	*pushed off circuit*
3	BMW Procar Championship Race	Monte Carlo	17/05/80	BS Fabrications	BMW M1	
3	MONACO GP	Monte Carlo	18/05/80	Parmalat Racing Team	Brabham BT49-Cosworth DFV	
3	Nürburgring 1000 Km	Nürburgring	25/05/80	BMW Motorsport GmbH	BMW M1	*c/d Hans Stuck*
ret	Spanish Grand Prix	Jarama	01/06/80	Parmalat Racing Team	Brabham BT49-Cosworth DFV	*gearbox/non-championship*
ret	BMW Procar Championship Race	Norisring	22/06/80	BS Fabrications	BMW M1	*collision with Pironi*
4	FRENCH GP	Paul Ricard	29/06/80	Parmalat Racing Team	Brabham BT49-Cosworth DFV	
2	BRITISH GP	Brands Hatch	13/07/80	Parmalat Racing Team	Brabham BT49-Cosworth DFV	
4	BMW Procar Championship Race	Hockenheim	09/08/80	BS Fabrications	BMW M1	
4	GERMAN GP	Hockenheim	10/08/80	Parmalat Racing Team	Brabham BT49-Cosworth DFV	
1	BMW Procar Championship Race	Österreichring	16/08/80	BS Fabrications	BMW M1	
5	AUSTRIAN GP	Österreichring	17/08/80	Parmalat Racing Team	Brabham BT49-Cosworth DFV	
1	BMW Procar Championship Race	Zandvoort	30/08/80	BS Fabrications	BMW M1	
1	DUTCH GP	Zandvoort	31/08/80	Parmalat Racing Team	Brabham BT49-Cosworth DFV	
1	BMW Procar Championship Race	Imola	13/09/80	BS Fabrications	BMW M1	*Pole/Fastest lap*
1	ITALIAN GP	Imola	14/09/80	Parmalat Racing Team	Brabham BT49-Cosworth DFV	
ret	CANADIAN GP	Montreal	28/09/80	Parmalat Racing Team	Brabham BT49-Cosworth DFV	*engine/Pole*
ret	US GP EAST	Watkins Glen	05/10/80	Parmalat Racing Team	Brabham BT49-Cosworth DFV	

1981

Pos	Race	Circuit	Date	Team	Car	Notes
2	South African Grand Prix	Kyalami	07/02/81	Parmalat Racing Team	Brabham BT49-Cosworth DFV	*Pole/non-championship*
3	US GP WEST	Long Beach	15/03/81	Parmalat Racing Team	Brabham BT49C-Cosworth DFV	
12	BRAZILIAN GP	Rio	29/03/81	Parmalat Racing Team	Brabham BT49C-Cosworth DFV	*slick tyres–wet race/Pole*
1	ARGENTINE GP	Buenos Aires	12/04/81	Parmalat Racing Team	Brabham BT49C-Cosworth DFV	*Pole/Fastest lap*
1	SAN MARINO GP	Imola	03/05/81	Parmalat Racing Team	Brabham BT49C-Cosworth DFV	
ret	BELGIAN GP	Zolder	17/05/81	Parmalat Racing Team	Brabham BT49C-Cosworth DFV	*collision with Jones*
1	Nürburgring 1000 Km	Nürburgring	24/05/81	Sauber Racing/BASF	BMW M1	*c/d Hans Stuck*
ret	MONACO GP	Monte Carlo	31/05/81	Parmalat Racing Team	Brabham BT49C-Cosworth DFV	*spun off/Pole*
ret	SPANISH GP	Jarama	21/06/81	Parmalat Racing Team	Brabham BT49C-Cosworth DFV	*spun off*
3	FRENCH GP	Dijon	05/07/81	Parmalat Racing Team	Brabham BT49C-Cosworth DFV	
ret	BRITISH GP	Silverstone	18/07/81	Parmalat Racing Team	Brabham BT49C-Cosworth DFV	*tyre failure–accident*
dns			18/07/81	Parmalat Racing Team	Brabham BT50-BMW M12/13	*practice only*
1	GERMAN GP	Hockenheim	02/08/81	Parmalat Racing Team	Brabham BT49C-Cosworth DFV	
3	AUSTRIAN GP	Österreichring	16/08/81	Parmalat Racing Team	Brabham BT49C-Cosworth DFV	
2	DUTCH GP	Zandvoort	30/08/81	Parmalat Racing Team	Brabham BT49C-Cosworth DFV	
6/*ret*	ITALIAN GP	Monza	13/09/81	Parmalat Racing Team	Brabham BT49C-Cosworth DFV	*engine*
5	CANADIAN GP	Montreal	27/09/81	Parmalat Racing Team	Brabham BT49C-Cosworth DFV	*Pole*
5	CAESAR'S PALACE GP	Las Vegas	17/10/81	Parmalat Racing Team	Brabham BT49C-Cosworth DFV	
2	Australian Grand Prix	Calder Park	07/11/81	Graham Watson	Ralt RT4-Ford	

1982

	Race	Circuit	Date	Team	Car	Notes
et	SOUTH AFRICAN GP	Kyalami	23/01/82	Parmalat Racing Team	Brabham BT50-BMW M12/13	spun off
sq	BRAZILIAN GP	Rio	21/03/82	Parmalat Racing Team	Brabham BT49D-Cosworth DFV	brake cooling tank/1st on road
et	US GP WEST	Long Beach	04/04/82	Parmalat Racing Team	Brabham BT49D-Cosworth DFV	soft brake pedal/hit wall
	BELGIAN GP	Zolder	09/05/82	Parmalat Racing Team	Brabham BT50-BMW M12/13	
et	MONACO GP	Monte Carlo	23/05/82	Parmalat Racing Team	Brabham BT50-BMW M12/13	gearbox
aq	US GP (DETROIT)	Detroit	06/06/82	Parmalat Racing Team	Brabham BT50-BMW M12/13	
	CANADIAN GP	Montreal	13/06/82	Parmalat Racing Team	Brabham BT50-BMW M12/13	
	DUTCH GP	Zandvoort	03/07/82	Parmalat Racing Team	Brabham BT50-BMW M12/13	
et	BRITISH GP	Brands Hatch	18/07/82	Parmalat Racing Team	Brabham BT50-BMW M12/13	fuel metering unit
et	FRENCH GP	Paul Ricard	25/07/82	Parmalat Racing Team	Brabham BT50-BMW M12/13	engine
et	GERMAN GP	Hockenheim	08/08/82	Parmalat Racing Team	Brabham BT50-BMW M12/13	hit by Salazar/Fastest lap
et	AUSTRIAN GP	Österreichring	15/08/82	Parmalat Racing Team	Brabham BT50-BMW M12/13	engine/Pole/Fastest lap
	SWISS GP	Dijon	29/08/82	Parmalat Racing Team	Brabham BT50-BMW M12/13	
t	ITALIAN GP	Monza	12/09/82	Parmalat Racing Team	Brabham BT50-BMW M12/13	clutch
et	CAESAR'S PALACE GP	Las Vegas	25/09/82	Parmalat Racing Team	Brabham BT50-BMW M12/13	spark plug
et	Australian Grand Prix	Calder Park	07/11/82	Goold Motorsport	Ralt RT4-Ford	multiple accident

1983

	Race	Circuit	Date	Team	Car	Notes
	BRAZILIAN GP	Rio	13/03/83	Fila Sport	Brabham BT52-BMW M12/13	Fastest lap
t	US GP WEST	Long Beach	27/03/83	Fila Sport	Brabham BT52-BMW M12/13	throttle
	FRENCH GP	Paul Ricard	17/04/83	Fila Sport	Brabham BT52-BMW M12/13	
t	SAN MARINO GP	Imola	01/05/83	Fila Sport	Brabham BT52-BMW M12/13	engine
	MONACO GP	Monte Carlo	15/05/83	Fila Sport	Brabham BT52-BMW M12/13	Fastest lap
	BELGIAN GP	Spa	22/05/83	Fila Sport	Brabham BT52-BMW M12/13	
	US GP (DETROIT)	Detroit	05/06/83	Fila Sport	Brabham BT52-BMW M12/13	
t	CANADIAN GP	Montreal	12/06/83	Fila Sport	Brabham BT52-BMW M12/13	throttle cable
	BRITISH GP	Silverstone	16/07/83	Fila Sport	Brabham BT52B-BMW M12/13	
/ret	GERMAN GP	Hockenheim	07/08/83	Fila Sport	Brabham BT52B-BMW M12/13	fire
	AUSTRIAN GP	Österreichring	14/08/83	Fila Sport	Brabham BT52B-BMW M12/13	
t	DUTCH GP	Zandvoort	28/08/83	Fila Sport	Brabham BT52B-BMW M12/13	collision with Prost/Pole
	ITALIAN GP	Monza	11/09/83	Fila Sport	Brabham BT52B-BMW M12/13	Fastest lap
	EUROPEAN GP	Brands Hatch	25/09/83	Fila Sport	Brabham BT52B-BMW M12/13	
	SOUTH AFRICAN GP	Kyalami	15/10/83	Fila Sport	Brabham BT52B-BMW M12/13	Fastest lap

1984

	Race	Circuit	Date	Team	Car	Notes
t	BRAZILIAN GP	Rio	25/03/84	Motor Racing Developments	Brabham BT53-BMW M12/13	engine
t	SOUTH AFRICAN GP	Kyalami	07/04/84	Motor Racing Developments	Brabham BT53-BMW M12/13	turbo compressor/Pole
/ret	BELGIAN GP	Zolder	29/04/84	Motor Racing Developments	Brabham BT53-BMW M12/13	engine
t	SAN MARINO GP	Imola	06/05/84	Motor Racing Developments	Brabham BT53-BMW M12/13	turbo/Pole/Fastest lap
t	FRENCH GP	Dijon	20/05/84	Motor Racing Developments	Brabham BT53-BMW M12/13	turbo
t	MONACO GP	Monte Carlo	03/06/84	Motor Racing Developments	Brabham BT53-BMW M12/13	water in electrics
	CANADIAN GP	Montreal	17/06/84	Motor Racing Developments	Brabham BT53-BMW M12/13	Pole/Fastest lap
	US GP (DETROIT)	Detroit	24/06/84	Motor Racing Developments	Brabham BT53-BMW M12/13	Pole
t	US GP (DALLAS)	Dallas	08/07/84	Motor Racing Developments	Brabham BT53-BMW M12/13	jammed throttle–hit wall
	BRITISH GP	Brands Hatch	22/07/84	Motor Racing Developments	Brabham BT53-BMW M12/13	turbo boost problems/Pole
t	GERMAN GP	Hockenheim	05/08/84	Motor Racing Developments	Brabham BT53-BMW M12/13	gearbox
	AUSTRIAN GP	Österreichring	19/08/84	Motor Racing Developments	Brabham BT53-BMW M12/13	Pole
	DUTCH GP	Zandvoort	26/08/84	Motor Racing Developments	Brabham BT53-BMW M12/13	oil pressure
	ITALIAN GP	Monza	09/09/84	Motor Racing Developments	Brabham BT53-BMW M12/13	engine/Pole
	EUROPEAN GP	Nürburgring	07/10/84	Motor Racing Developments	Brabham BT53-BMW M12/13	Pole/Fastest lap
	PORTUGUESE GP	Estoril	21/10/84	Motor Racing Developments	Brabham BT53-BMW M12/13	spin/Pole

1985

	Race	Circuit	Date	Team	Car	Notes
	BRAZILIAN GP	Rio	07/04/85	Motor Racing Developments	Brabham BT54-BMW M12/13	transmission
	PORTUGUESE GP	Estoril	21/04/85	Motor Racing Developments	Brabham BT54-BMW M12/13	tyres/handling
et	SAN MARINO GP	Imola	05/05/85	Motor Racing Developments	Brabham BT54-BMW M12/13	out of fuel
	MONACO GP	Monte Carlo	19/05/85	Motor Racing Developments	Brabham BT54-BMW M12/13	accident with Patrese
	CANADIAN GP	Montreal	16/06/85	Motor Racing Developments	Brabham BT54-BMW M12/13	transmission
	US GP (DETROIT)	Detroit	23/06/85	Motor Racing Developments	Brabham BT54-BMW M12/13	
	FRENCH GP	Paul Ricard	07/07/85	Motor Racing Developments	Brabham BT54-BMW M12/13	
	BRITISH GP	Silverstone	21/07/85	Motor Racing Developments	Brabham BT54-BMW M12/13	
	GERMAN GP	Nürburgring	04/08/85	Motor Racing Developments	Brabham BT54-BMW M12/13	turbo
	AUSTRIAN GP	Österreichring	18/08/85	Motor Racing Developments	Brabham BT54-BMW M12/13	exhaust
	DUTCH GP	Zandvoort	25/08/85	Motor Racing Developments	Brabham BT54-BMW M12/13	stalled on grid/Pole
	ITALIAN GP	Monza	08/09/85	Motor Racing Developments	Brabham BT54-BMW M12/13	
	BELGIAN GP	Spa	15/09/85	Motor Racing Developments	Brabham BT54-BMW M12/13	
	EUROPEAN GP	Brands Hatch	06/10/85	Motor Racing Developments	Brabham BT54-BMW M12/13	hit spinning Rosberg
	SOUTH AFRICAN GP	Kyalami	19/10/85	Motor Racing Developments	Brabham BT54-BMW M12/13	engine
	AUSTRALIAN GP	Adelaide	03/11/85	Motor Racing Developments	Brabham BT54-BMW M12/13	electrical fire

1986

1	BRAZILIAN GP	Rio	23/03/86	Canon Williams Honda Team	Williams FW11-Honda RA166-E	*Fastest lap*
ret	SPANISH GP	Jerez	13/04/86	Canon Williams Honda Team	Williams FW11-Honda RA166-E	*overheating/engine*
2	SAN MARINO GP	Imola	27/04/86	Canon Williams Honda Team	Williams FW11-Honda RA166-E	*Fastest lap*
7	MONACO GP	Monte Carlo	11/05/86	Canon Williams Honda Team	Williams FW11-Honda RA166-E	
ret	BELGIAN GP	Spa	25/05/86	Canon Williams Honda Team	Williams FW11-Honda RA166-E	*turbo boost control/Pole*
3	CANADIAN GP	Montreal	15/06/86	Canon Williams Honda Team	Williams FW11-Honda RA166-E	*Fastest lap*
ret	US GP (DETROIT)	Detroit	22/06/86	Canon Williams Honda Team	Williams FW11-Honda RA166-E	*hit chicane/Fastest lap*
3	FRENCH GP	Paul Ricard	06/07/86	Canon Williams Honda Team	Williams FW11-Honda RA166-E	
2	BRITISH GP	Brands Hatch	13/07/86	Canon Williams Honda Team	Williams FW11-Honda RA166-E	*Pole*
1	GERMAN GP	Hockenheim	27/07/86	Canon Williams Honda Team	Williams FW11-Honda RA166-E	
1	HUNGARIAN GP	Hungaroring	10/08/86	Canon Williams Honda Team	Williams FW11-Honda RA166-E	*Fastest lap*
ret	AUSTRIAN GP	Österreichring	17/08/86	Canon Williams Honda Team	Williams FW11-Honda RA166-E	*engine*
1	ITALIAN GP	Monza	07/09/86	Canon Williams Honda Team	Williams FW11-Honda RA166-E	
3	PORTUGUESE GP	Estoril	21/09/86	Canon Williams Honda Team	Williams FW11-Honda RA166-E	
4	MEXICAN GP	Mexico City	12/10/86	Canon Williams Honda Team	Williams FW11-Honda RA166-E	*Fastest lap*
2	AUSTRALIAN GP	Adelaide	26/10/86	Canon Williams Honda Team	Williams FW11-Honda RA166-E	*pit stop–tyres/Fastest lap*

1987

2	BRAZILIAN GP	Rio	12/04/87	Canon Williams Honda Team	Williams FW11B-Honda RA166-E	*Fastest lap*
dns	SAN MARINO GP	Imola	03/05/87	Canon Williams Honda Team	Williams FW11B-Honda RA167-G	*accident in practice*
ret	BELGIAN GP	Spa	17/05/87	Canon Williams Honda Team	Williams FW11B-Honda RA167-G	*turbo sensor*
2	MONACO GP	Monte Carlo	31/05/87	Canon Williams Honda Team	Williams FW11B-Honda RA167-G	
2	US GP (DETROIT)	Detroit	21/06/87	Canon Williams Honda Team	Williams FW11B-Honda RA167-G	
2	FRENCH GP	Paul Ricard	05/07/87	Canon Williams Honda	Williams FW11B-Honda RA167-G	*Fastest lap*
2	BRITISH GP	Silverstone	12/07/87	Canon Williams Honda	Williams FW11B-Honda RA167-G	*Pole*
1	GERMAN GP	Hockenheim	26/07/87	Canon Williams Honda	Williams FW11B-Honda RA167-G	
1	HUNGARIAN GP	Hungaroring	09/08/87	Canon Williams Honda	Williams FW11B-Honda RA167-G	*Fastest lap*
2	AUSTRIAN GP	Österreichring	16/08/87	Canon Williams Honda	Williams FW11B-Honda RA167-G	*Pole*
1	ITALIAN GP	Monza	06/09/87	Canon Williams Honda	Williams FW11B-Honda RA167-G	*Pole*
3	PORTUGUESE GP	Estoril	20/09/87	Canon Williams Honda	Williams FW11B-Honda RA167-C	
4	SPANISH GP	Jerez	27/09/87	Canon Williams Honda	Williams FW11B-Honda RA167-G	*pit stop–tyres/Pole*
2	MEXICAN GP	Mexico City	18/10/87	Canon Williams Honda	Williams FW11B-Honda RA167-G	*Fastest lap*
15/ret	JAPANESE GP	Suzuka	01/11/87	Canon Williams Honda	Williams FW11B-Honda RA167-G	*engine*
ret	AUSTRALIAN GP	Adelaide	15/11/87	Canon Williams Honda	Williams FW11B-Honda RA167-G	*brakes/gear linkage*

1988

3	BRAZILIAN GP	Rio	03/04/88	Camel Team Lotus Honda	Lotus 100T-Honda RA168-E	
3	SAN MARINO GP	Imola	01/05/88	Camel Team Lotus Honda	Lotus 100T-Honda RA168-E	
ret	MONACO GP	Monte Carlo	15/05/88	Camel Team Lotus Honda	Lotus 100T-Honda RA168-E	*collision with Warwick*
ret	MEXICAN GP	Mexico City	29/05/88	Camel Team Lotus Honda	Lotus 100T-Honda RA168-E	*engine*
4	CANADIAN GP	Montreal	12/06/88	Camel Team Lotus Honda	Lotus 100T-Honda RA168-E	*handling problems*
ret	US GP (DETROIT)	Detroit	19/06/88	Camel Team Lotus Honda	Lotus 100T-Honda RA168-E	*spun off*
5	FRENCH GP	Paul Ricard	03/07/88	Camel Team Lotus Honda	Lotus 100T-Honda RA168-E	
5	BRITISH GP	Silverstone	10/07/88	Camel Team Lotus Honda	Lotus 100T-Honda RA168-E	
ret	GERMAN GP	Hockenheim	24/07/88	Camel Team Lotus Honda	Lotus 100T-Honda RA168-E	*spun off*
8	HUNGARIAN GP	Hungaroring	07/08/88	Camel Team Lotus Honda	Lotus 100T-Honda RA168-E	*hit Martini–pit stop*
6	BELGIAN GP	Spa	28/08/88	Camel Team Lotus Honda	Lotus 100T-Honda RA168-E	
ret	ITALIAN GP	Monza	11/09/88	Camel Team Lotus Honda	Lotus 100T-Honda RA168-E	*clutch–spun off*
ret	PORTUGUESE GP	Estoril	25/09/88	Camel Team Lotus Honda	Lotus 100T-Honda RA168-E	*clutch*
8	SPANISH GP	Jerez	02/10/88	Camel Team Lotus Honda	Lotus 100T-Honda RA168-E	*pit stop–tyres*
ret	JAPANESE GP	Suzuka	30/10/88	Camel Team Lotus Honda	Lotus 100T-Honda RA168-E	*unwell*
3	AUSTRALIAN GP	Adelaide	13/11/88	Camel Team Lotus Honda	Lotus 100T-Honda RA168-E	

1989

ret	BRAZILIAN GP	Rio	26/03/89	Camel Team Lotus	Lotus 101-Judd CV	*fuel pump*
ret	SAN MARINO GP	Imola	23/04/89	Camel Team Lotus	Lotus 101-Judd CV	*engine*
ret	MONACO GP	Monte Carlo	07/05/89	Camel Team Lotus	Lotus 101-Judd CV	*accident with de Cesaris*
11	MEXICAN GP	Mexico City	28/05/89	Camel Team Lotus	Lotus 101-Judd CV	
ret	US GP (PHOENIX)	Phoenix	04/06/89	Camel Team Lotus	Lotus 101-Judd CV	*hit wall*
4	CANADIAN GP	Montreal	18/06/89	Camel Team Lotus	Lotus 101-Judd CV	
8	FRENCH GP	Paul Ricard	09/07/89	Camel Team Lotus	Lotus 101-Judd CV	*handling problems*
4	BRITISH GP	Silverstone	16/07/89	Camel Team Lotus	Lotus 101-Judd CV	
5	GERMAN GP	Hockenheim	30/07/89	Camel Team Lotus	Lotus 101-Judd CV	
6	HUNGARIAN GP	Hungaroring	13/08/89	Camel Team Lotus	Lotus 101-Judd CV	
dnq	BELGIAN GP	Spa	27/08/89	Camel Team Lotus	Lotus 101-Judd CV	
ret	ITALIAN GP	Monza	10/09/89	Camel Team Lotus	Lotus 101-Judd CV	*spun off*
ret	PORTUGUESE GP	Estoril	24/09/89	Camel Team Lotus	Lotus 101-Judd CV	*collision with Caffi*
8	SPANISH GP	Jerez	01/10/89	Camel Team Lotus	Lotus 101-Judd CV	
4	JAPANESE GP	Suzuka	22/10/89	Camel Team Lotus	Lotus 101-Judd CV	
ret	AUSTRALIAN GP	Adelaide	05/11/89	Camel Team Lotus	Lotus 101-Judd CV	*hit Ghinzani*

1990

US GP (PHOENIX)	Phoenix	11/03/90	Benetton Formula	Benetton B189-Ford HA	*pit stop-tyres/brake problem*
BRAZILIAN GP	Interlagos	25/03/90	Benetton Formula	Benetton B189-Ford HA	*two pit stops-tyres*
SAN MARINO GP	Imola	13/05/90	Benetton Formula	Benetton B190-Ford HA	*collision with Alesi*
sq MONACO GP	Monte Carlo	27/05/90	Benetton Formula	Benetton B190-Ford HA	*black-flagged–push-start*
CANADIAN GP	Montreal	10/06/90	Benetton Formula	Benetton B190-Ford HA	
MEXICAN GP	Mexico City	24/06/90	Benetton Formula	Benetton B190-Ford HA	*tyre vibration–pit stop*
FRENCH GP	Paul Ricard	08/07/90	Benetton Formula	Benetton B190-Ford HA	*pit stop–tyres*
BRITISH GP	Silverstone	15/07/90	Benetton Formula	Benetton B190-Ford HB	*had to start at back of grid*
t GERMAN GP	Hockenheim	29/07/90	Benetton Formula	Benetton B190-Ford HB	*engine*
HUNGARIAN GP	Hungaroring	12/08/90	Benetton Formula	Benetton B190-Ford HB	
BELGIAN GP	Spa	26/08/90	Benetton Formula	Benetton B190-Ford HB	*used spare car/no clutch*
ITALIAN GP	Monza	09/09/90	Benetton Formula	Benetton B190-Ford HB	*puncture–pit stop*
PORTUGUESE GP	Estoril	23/09/90	Benetton Formula	Benetton B190-Ford HB	*pit stop–tyres*
t SPANISH GP	Jerez	30/09/90	Benetton Formula	Benetton B190-Ford HB	*electrics*
JAPANESE GP	Suzuka	21/10/90	Benetton Formula	Benetton B190-Ford HB	
AUSTRALIAN GP	Adelaide	04/11/90	Benetton Formula	Benetton B190-Ford HB	

Formula 1 World Championship positions/points (1979-90)

Year	Position	Points	Year	Position	Points	Year	Position	Points
1979	15th=	3	1983	1st	59	1987	1st	76
1980	2nd	54	1984	5th	29	1988	6th	22
1981	1st	50	1985	8th	21	1989	8th	12
1982	11th	20	1986	3rd	69	1990	3rd	44
								459

Formula 1 World Championship placings
1st–6th + Pole + Fastest lap (1979-90)

1st	2nd	3rd	4th	5th	6th	Pole	Fastest lap
22	20	15	17	12	7	24	23

*Brazilian fans have had to divide their loyalties since
the arrival of Senna, but here at Kyalami in 1983 they
carry their hero's banner high.*